Turning Around the Heart

Stories of Possibility, Connection, and Transformation

Cindy Chicoine

*Linda —
To one who
knows & lives
the teaching
stories.
Cindy*

Accompanied by Meditations, Reflection Questions
and Journal Prompts For Individuals and Groups

Shapato Publishing, LLC
Everly, Iowa

Published by: Shapato Publishing, LLC
                PO Box 476
                Everly, Iowa 51338

ISBN 978-0983352693
Library of Congress Control Number: 2012953352

First Printing November 2012

Illustrations by Guy Kyar

"We are living our own stories every minute of every day, but how do we recognize those stories and how do we learn the lessons they are trying to teach? Cindy Chicoine offers the answers to those questions in her new book, "Turning Around The Heart." With her instructive and inspiring stories, study exercises, and meditations, she provides a path of understanding and a precise guide to the power of story in our lives. I highly recommend this book."

James A. Autry
Author, *Choosing Gratitude; Learning To Love The Life You Have.*

***

"Cindy Chicoine's teaching tales and meditations are perfect illustrations of the power of story to heal and guide. Her book is a valuable resource for anyone ready to harvest the events of their lives and mine them for the wisdom they carry. A great body-mind-spirit approach to healing and transformation."

Jan Phillips
Author, *No Ordinary Time*

***

"Stories have a way of bypassing our often critical minds and dropping us into our hearts. Cindy Chicoine's inspiring new book; *Turning Around the Heart,* does exactly that - allows us to feel our hearts open in beautiful and meaningful ways. The transformational stories, exercises and processes allow us to transform, grow and remember who we really are. With stories that are deep, funny, and insightful, she backs up each one with exercises, and meditations for the reader to process how each story affected them. *Turning Around the Heart* is a must-read for anyone on the path of inspiration and transformation."

Karen Drucker
Singer/Songwriter/Author of *Let Go of the Shore.*

This book is dedicated to:

The teaching stories living in and around us all.

I extend a special thank you to all who have contributed to these teaching stories. Even in cases where permission has been given, I have deliberately changed identifying information while maintaining the integrity of the message. Though your name, profession, location, story elements and, in some cases, gender has been changed and your story may have been combined with one or more others, please know that your stories have blessed and taught me and, I hope, now, will teach many others.

*If you have been processing traumatic memories please only use the meditations with caution and perhaps involve a therapist trained in traumatic memory work!

INTRODUCTION

A Hundred Teaching Stories

Her words still resonate in my soul: "The indigenous cultures believe that if you have a hundred teaching stories you are a shaman or a healer." And that's where the story of *this* story began. I was changed the day Angeles Arrien, cultural anthropologist, author, and master storyteller impressed upon me, during that conference many years ago, that stories have power, healing power. I felt as though my higher consciousness was soaking up all the goodies, much of it through story. Those ancient cultures know the value of story to bring healing on very deep levels.

I believe we are all healers. I believe we all have an inner healer residing within us. I also believe we are all storytellers. I believe we all carry healing potentiality in our stories. Yes, of course, we can be caught and stuck in some of our stories where we have been wounded, but those are often the very places and the very stories where we could harvest a teaching that might be life changing. For me teaching stories are those that carry deep meaning, take us to a profound place of understanding or awareness, and help us remember the truth of who we are, our authenticity. Those kinds of teaching stories can bring healing on some very core levels rather than reinforcing our woundedness.

I have often witnessed the amazing resilience we carry within since I began journeying in an intentional way with people of all ages and of different cultures in the 1970s. I believe that one potent way we can access that amazing resilience within is through the doorway of teaching stories. Large cultural stories hold healing, others stories can hold healing, and our stories, our experiences, may hold the greatest healing potential for us if we can hear them, feel them, see them from that inner healer place that lives within.

Several years ago I had a dream, a vision, really, that I would write a book. I felt the truth of that dream message as a calling. While I knew the importance of this message, I tucked it away, as we often do, because I was busy. I thought I didn't have time to concentrate on writing a book. Then, I was diagnosed with breast cancer. My prognosis is excellent. But that experience woke me up and I took a serious look at what I want to accomplish before I die. I made my "bucket list." On that list was this book.

I don't have a hundred stories here. What I do have are some teaching stories from both my personal and professional life. All of them have opened up new possibilities, new ways of seeing or being; have bridged a connection with others, with parts of myself, or with a larger view of things; and have transformed me, are still transforming me. And so, I offer you these teaching stories in whatever way they may hold for you the energy of possibility, connection and transformation.

At the end of each story are optional reflection questions, journal prompts and meditations. There may also be other suggested activities. You may wish to purchase a new journal or notebook to accompany you through these stories. Or you may feel called to use your existing journal. However you choose to record your reactions and experiences with these stories, they are all being offered to invite a deepening of your experience with the themes and to support you in harvesting your own meaning from the story.

But more than this, these stories and the questions and activities that follow are meant to be an invitation; an invitation to recover, claim and live *your* teaching stories, to harvest the healing in them and allow them to offer you possibility, connection, and transformation.

I invite you now through the doorway of story. As you read these stories perhaps you will be entertained by them. Perhaps you will connect to your own story through them. Just notice. Notice if there are things in the story that resonate with your life. Notice if certain things touch you or invite you to a larger view. And as you live your life, as you journey through whatever chapters of your story you are called to, I invite you to listen to your life unfolding with the ears of your heart. I invite you to see the experiences in your life with the eyes of your deeper self. I invite you to be present so that you may hear the teaching stories of your life. I invite you to notice the themes, the meaning, and the ways in which your stories touch the deepest core of you and bring healing. I invite you to the healing presence of story in your own life.

Perhaps you will be with this book on your own. Perhaps you will enter into these stories with a sacred circle within your own community. Perhaps you will carry them into your book club. Perhaps you will share your process with a friend, a therapist, a spiritual director.

There is no right or wrong way to be with these stories, or your own stories, there is only your own wonderful way. The doorway of story is open.

As you enter, may it bring you all that you need.

"The breezes at dawn have secrets to tell you.
Don't go back to sleep.
You must ask for what you really want.
Don't go back to sleep.
People are going back and forth across the doorsill where
the two worlds touch.
The door is round and open.
Don't go back to sleep."

Rumi
12th century Sufi poet

"Remember only this one thing," said Badger. "The stories people tell have a way of taking care of them. If stories come to you, care for them. And learn to give them away where they are needed. Sometimes a person needs a story more than food to stay alive; that is why we put these stories in each other's memory. This is how people care for themselves."

Crow and Weasel by Barry Lopez

CONTENTS

Turning Around the Heart

Stories of Possibility, Connection, and Transformation

PART ONE:

Turning Around the Heart of Possibility

We open to what is possible. When we are willing to move through our life storms, real or imagined, when we allow ourselves to become still and to be seen, when we surrender ourselves into something larger than our human self it is then that we may find what is possible. Perhaps this takes us into the magic of surprise, being held, integration, being polished, or receiving what we need. Perhaps through this we bring possibility to others. Perhaps we find ourselves able to *be* all that we are called to be.

WAITING

Magic happens. Dreams, long buried, those often carried closest to the heart, can become reality. There can be countless challenges along the way but if we hold steadfast to these dreams, if we wait until the ripe time, the Universe provides, things somehow fall into place. We return to these dreams, we remember, and we enter into the unfolding magic.

Here are three stories of such magic:

My partner, Morgan, has held a dream for many years. She has always wanted to study Five Element Acupuncture, the Taoist-focused style of acupuncture. Yet there were always plenty of reasons to delay such a large undertaking. There was the money and time. There was the fact that only one school in the United States taught this style of acupuncture, it was in Colorado, and we were in Iowa. There were prerequisite courses to take even before admission. While some of the studies could be done long distance, once she was admitted to the program, it meant several extended trips to Colorado over a two-year period and after that she would need to live there to complete 15 months of supervised clinical work before graduation. It meant challenging her fears that a nearly 60-year-old brain could learn all these new things and then successfully pass the exams for licensure in our state. Of course, there was my own hesitancy. No small thing let me tell you. How would I manage our household alone through a Midwest winter requiring snow removal? How would all the yard work be done in the warmer months? How would we keep our relationship strong with such distance? Could I juggle all this and maintain my own busy practice?

In spite of all this, Morgan held that dream until the time was just right. She entered the several-year journey, jumped through all the hoops, completed all the studies and requirements, passed all the exams and learned a whole new way of supporting the health of her clients. Now, with the license on her wall she leaves for the office in the morning with a bounce in her step. She returns home at the end of the day with joy and a deep sense of satisfaction. In between she is a partner with clients in new and powerful ways.

≈

The Anderson family had four small children all under the age of six and was in need of in-home assistance from our social services agency. They lived at the very edge of the city and the neighbors in the adjoining suburb would often call Human Services to report that one of the middle-aged boys was walking down the street without proper clothing for the season. My colleague and I, working as a team, were called in to evaluate the family's needs, offer parent-skill coaching and education, and ultimately get them back on track so their children could remain safe and at home.

What became clear from the outset was that the mom, Alice, was completely overwhelmed and the dad, Jake, who was home on disability, was severely depressed. Alice needed all the support she could get and responded with great joy to trained volunteer babysitters who gave her a break. She then had more energy to parent and to try to implement the new parenting skills we taught her. We coordinated the re-evaluation and adjustment of Jake's medication and while it made a slight difference, even after a couple of months, Jake remained distant and withdrawn. That is, until the day a conversation about hopes and dreams elicited new information—even for Alice—about Jake.

Jake had always been enthralled by trees and forestry. As a boy, his dad would take him into the nearby woods and they would hike for an afternoon of quiet time and quiet conversation. His dad would share his knowledge of trees and botany while Jake would listen with rapture. It was a time of father-son bonding, a time where they both left all their cares behind. As a child, Jake dreamed of running his own tree farm. Then, the years passed, children came, health challenges arose, stress and bills mounted up, and life moved faster and faster. Jake hadn't been hiking in many years and the dream of running his own tree farm had been shelved long ago. And then, the year before we met Jake, his dad, his first hiking buddy, died. With his death, Jake's dream also died.

And yet . . . Jake came alive as he shared this old dream and his hiking experiences with his dad. His gaze met ours, his voice sounded more like a song than the monotone we'd grown used to, and you could feel the air alive with something like excitement, something their house had been without for a long time. Eventually, a plan to resurrect Jake's dream was formed and Jake began to address his grief for his father not by talking about his dad and his feelings but through step-by-step action on that dream.

The first step was cleaning out the small yard shed, which would become the office and storage place for the tree farm. That was a job but, with support, Jake rallied and worked steadily hauling out the junk, painting, and making the minor repairs necessary. The kids loved being part of this and Jake and Alice did too. Next was the process to obtain the county's approval to use the dozen extra acres at the edge of his property for the small tree farm. Eventually all the forms were complete and the permits were granted. Jake and Alice researched the business skills needed and studied the overall cost requirements. In the settling of his father's estate, Jake had been left just enough money to get the farm going with tilling the soil, a few trees and the necessary equipment. Miraculously, the very neighbors who were most concerned about Jake and Alice's family began to donate garden and pruning equipment. They even volunteered some sweat equity. What had felt like judgment to Jake and Alice had shifted to cooperation and encouragement. A sense of community was forming. One retired neighbor even offered to mentor Jake in the business end of this dream and Jake was delighted to accept. Day by day, those extra acres were transformed and Jake came alive as he inched closer to the dream he'd held inside for so many years.

Though our services had become less and less needed, we were there on that wondrous day when the dream became reality. The freshly painted sign hung proud as people began to come for the grand opening and those first few trees were sold. The first two, though, were handed to us by Jake. The feathery needles of those white pines, in bright painted yellow containers, danced in the afternoon breeze. Yellow, Jake explained had always been, for him, the color of hope.

As those tiny trees swayed gently in the backseat as we drove away that day, my colleague and I were silent, both in awe at the power of a recovered dream, of the life inside a dream that lay dormant for many years, and at the power of waiting with hope, even if some might call it unreasonable hope. This recovered hope nourished Jake's whole family for years to come.

≈

I have written stories for years. Maybe it would be more accurate to say that stories have written through me for years. Periodically, I would think about maybe, perhaps, one day putting the stories all together in a book. I even had a dream that I would write a book. Then life happens, and mine has been full and rich, so the thought continued to be "one day."

In the summer of 2010, I attended a women's retreat with Karen Drucker, an immensely talented musician, workshop leader, and an all-around amazing person. During breakfast one morning, she asked what was happening in my life and somehow the topic of my stories came up. She was pretty blunt about it.

"Get off your behind and get going on this dream," she said.

I knew she was right. And so I began compiling the Post-it® Notes that held little story promptings and flushed out those stories. I polished some stories that had been written long ago and found many new stories waiting to be written, too. I began learning about what it takes to actually write a book. And I had to schedule time, lots of time, to do this amidst an already full life. It had been a calling that I heard, and ignored, for many years. Though it felt both exhilarating and daunting, I was immensely thankful that the Universe, in all her wisdom, gave me the nudges I needed.

≈

It is said that a lotus flower seed can wait many years, even a hundred, before being planted and still have the life inside of it to grow. Way past what we think may be possible, life waits with us for that planting. Jake and his family were evidence of that. My partner, Morgan is evidence of that. And the words you are reading now are evidence of that, too.

Reflection Questions and Journal Prompts

- *What, if anything, speaks to you from these stories?*

- *What stories do you have about holding your dream and hope seeds until the time was right to plant them? What were your reasons for waiting? What support from your inner self or others helped the planting of those dream seeds? What was it like for your body/mind/emotion and spirit to tend those long-waiting seeds?*

- *What dreams of yours are still waiting to be planted? Why are you still waiting? What is the cost of waiting? What would it take for you to plant these seeds and nurture them to flower? What is a single step you could take to begin this process as a way of preparing the soil?*

Suggested Activities or Experiences

- *Maybe you want to get some seeds from your local garden center and have them symbolize real dreams and hopes you are holding. See what it would be like to plant, tend and watch those seeds grow.*

- *Allow yourself some creative expression of yourself as a lotus seed being planted and growing after all these years. This could take the form of sculpting, drawing, painting, dancing or writing. Just notice how that expression is for your mind/body/emotion and spirit.*

The following lyrics from a song by Kristy Hanson are part of a chant I learned many years ago. Maybe you will find this song and sing this part of it. Maybe you will be called to make your own song of waiting, returning, planting and growing your dreams. Maybe you will sing this to your seeds.

> "She's been waiting, waiting,
> She's been waiting so long.
> She's been waiting for her children
> To remember to return."

Meditation for Dream Seeds

Begin by finding a comfortable place to sit or lie down where you won't be disturbed. Allow your awareness to come to your breath. For now, just notice the breath. In and out, in and out. Just breathe. Let the breath breathe you. Be breathed by the breath. Take all the time you need right now to just be with the breath.

And when you are ready, you welcome your body into this moment, into this experience. Begin by bringing loving awareness to the body. Just notice the body and how it is at this moment, of this day. There is no need to change anything and there is no judgment, only loving awareness of the body. Notice any places of tension, discomfort or holding. Notice any places of ease, flow and comfort in the body. Welcome the body into this experience, this day and breathe a breath of acceptance to the body. Only after extending awareness, welcome and acceptance to the body do you notice if there is any tension, holding or energy in the body, that is no longer needed, that is ready to be released. If so, then you just let it go, perhaps sailing it out on the exhaled breath. And if this created any new spaciousness in the body, you can use your breath to expand out the health and wholeness that lives at your core into this newly opened space. You may also wish to partner that with breathing in the wholeness energy available in the larger universe outside of you. Breathing in, and expanding out health and wholeness for the body.

You can extend this same welcome to the emotion self. Begin by noticing with loving awareness whatever emotions are present with you this moment of this day. No judgment, no right or wrong, no need to change anything. For now just notice the emotion self. Welcome the emotion self into this day. When you are ready, breathe a breath of acceptance to the emotion self no matter what is found there. And only after this welcoming and this extending of acceptance do you notice if there is any emotion energy that is no longer needed that is ready to be released. And if there is, you just let it go. No force, no effort, just release. Perhaps you send it out with the support of the exhaled breath. Release it in whatever is your way. And if this has created any new spaciousness in your emotion self you expand out the emotional health and wholeness that lives at your core into this newly opened space. You may also wish to partner this with breathing in the larger

emotion health and wholeness energy available from the larger universe outside of you. Breathe in and expand out to fill the emotion self with health and wholeness.

You can give this same gift now to your thinking mind. Taking time to pause and notice with loving awareness the thoughts and beliefs moving through the mind along with noticing any mental chatter present at this moment of this day. Pausing to notice the thoughts without the need to engage them and perhaps remembering that the thoughts are not necessarily your deeper truths. After a few moments of noticing, you welcome your thinking mind into this day and this experience. Breathe a breath of acceptance to your mind. And only after noticing, welcoming and extending acceptance, do you notice if there are any old beliefs that are no longer true for you or any mental chatter or thoughts that are no longer needed. If there are, and they are ready to be released, you just let them go. Perhaps with the support of your exhaled breath or whatever is your way. And if this creates any new spaciousness in your mind, you expand out the peace and wholeness that lives at your core to fill this space. Again, you may wish to partner this with the peace and harmony that also lives in the world outside of you. Breathing in and expanding out peace and harmony for the mind.

Now you have created an environment where your wisest Self can emerge. And so you pause and breathe and be as this Self that is your true nature. You take all the time you need deepening your connection as this wise and expansive Self.

As always, you may remain here relaxing with your wisest Self. Or, you may choose to come on a journey of planting a dream-seed.

If you are choosing to journey, you now find yourself outdoors in a place that is safe and nurturing for you. You notice the environment and are aware of how pleasing it is to all your senses. To your delight you find that in your pocket is a seed that you have been carrying for a long time. You have nearly forgotten this seed but here it is.

Just now you see a sign that points to a fertile place where long-held seeds can be planted. Something deep inside you decides to go to this place. Along the way you may be joined by other helpers. You may be joined by others on the way to plant their seeds. You may journey alone. You trust that in whatever way you journey, that it is just right for you.

You arrive at this place of fertility with your seed. You are amazed at the lushness of this place. All that you need to plant this seed is available to you. All that you need to nourish and tend this seed into growth is available to you. All that you need to harvest the gifts of this seed are also available.

In your own way and time, with all that you need, you reach into your pocket and bring out your precious seed. You may gaze at this seed with love. You may have full knowledge of what kind of seed this is and what will grow from it. You may realize that this awareness will unfold over time. You feel deep trust either way. You may find a pre-planting ritual unfolding. You may be ready to just plant this seed. The perfect process of planting your seed now happens. With full presence, you plant your seed.

You notice how it feels to have rediscovered this seed and planted it. You notice how it feels to trust the potency of this seed. You notice how it feels to claim all that you need to tend this seed into life. You notice how it feels to know that what is needed now for this seed is available and you welcome and receive it all.

As you prepare to leave this place you know that you will return as needed, you will tend as needed, and you will harvest as needed.

You return now to the beginning of the path you have first taken, feeling a sense of satisfaction. At the path's beginning you pause to express your gratitude.

When you are ready you begin to bring your awareness back to the place where you first began this meditation. You breathe deeply and feel your body supported by the surface that holds it. When you are ready you open your eyes and bring your full consciousness back to your present environment.

You may wish to journal about your experience or share with a trusted friend.

STILL SECRET TO US

Wispy brown bangs hid deep, sorrowful eyes. Many days she hung out on the periphery in that folded-in-on-herself way. One day, she rode the steam of an audible deep breath to approach me when the coast was clear. Janie was a freshman in high school and I was a junior. She began to share a story of financial and relational poverty, of past abuse and neglect.

Nearly every week now, she would find me and share more and deeper. In my heart, I allowed the finding. Janie found me physically, yes. But more than that, she found the inner guide within me, which then had no name. She taught me about the power of being present, of witnessing, of how, through deep listening, wisdom is voiced, burdens released and way made for joy.

One day, later that year, standing tall with eyes visible and filled with tears, Janie spoke. "Because of how you listen to me, I now know that I can be happy. I am free to be me."

And she was. And I am . . . grateful for her naming of my call to this kind of listening ministry.

Two hearts. Two lives. Two Discoveries.

≈

When we grow up feeling as if we are a bit of an oddball, slightly off the norm, it's important to have people who *get* us, who see us in some way that maybe we can't even see ourselves yet. Patrice, a longtime family friend, was one of those people for me. Patrice and her husband, Robert, raised nine children in our community. Those children were similar ages to my siblings and I. My parents socialized with Patrice and her husband. Yet with all her responsibilities and the many things that occupied her, Patrice nurtured, cared about, and asked me about my life and especially my counseling work. We shared a love of offering support to those who were hurting or struggling, both formally through our work and informally in our personal lives.

During my growing up years, my family had been the recipient of Patrice and her husband, Robert's, great kindnesses. Their concern was particularly evident as my father was dying from cancer.

One day, they were at the hospital offering support as we all sensed that dad was close to death. I was crying copious tears and Patrice pulled out these king-size Kleenex and gave them to me. *Jackpot! King-size Kleenex!*

On the surface this seemed a simple thing, but it touched a deep place in me. I felt it as one more sign of her seeing me, getting me, knowing me as a deeply sensitive person, as one who cries, as one who struggled for many years to make peace with my tears.

In that simple act of giving me some king-size Kleenex, I felt as if Patrice said to me, "I honor your tears and your grief, and no matter how big it is, it can be held."

A few years after my dad died, Patrice died, too. I wasn't able to attend her services but I sent this story to be read at her visitation. I offered it humbly to her family with the wish that they would know that I honored their tears and their grief. With the wish that they would know that no matter how big their grief was, it could be held. A very wise woman taught me that lesson.

Two losses. Two times the mourning. Two boxes of giant-size Kleenex.

≈

Darin was a regular presence at my childhood church. He radiated warmth through his quiet demeanor. Years passed and I knew very little about his life and family, yet I enjoyed our brief encounters and his "fully-present" hugs.

Then one week we were sharing the journey to the parking lot and started talking. I asked Darrin, who was now retired, what he had done for a living.

"It's kind of a long and winding story," he said.

"I love stories," I replied.

Darrin had worked for the local office of a vitamin supplement company. One day, his boss told him about a customer, several counties away, who was having problems with his livestock. The boss told Darrin to go out to the customer's farm and solve the problem. Darrin was surprised, "Who me?"

"Yes, you," replied his boss. "I think you are just the person to do this."

Feeling uncertain and worried about his ability to solve this large concern, Darrin reluctantly agreed to go. He believed he lacked the necessary training and knowledge to solve this customer's concern, so was surprised when he got to the customer's farm and found that he just knew what was called for. He made his recommendation to the client and then came to find out that this was the perfect solution. The customer's livestock responded with such success that Darrin was sent out on similar consultations. Before long, he became known for his gift in solving complex livestock concerns and ultimately traveled far-and-wide sharing that gift.

"How much of that first visit was intuition?" I asked.

Smiling in his humble way, Darrin answered, "A lot of it. Really, quite a lot."

"Wow," I said," your boss saw something in you, didn't he?"

"He sure did," said Paul.

Two men. Two talents. Two discoveries.

≈

These stories illustrate how sometimes, when we are fortunate, others see something in us that we can't yet see. They believe in us in a way that we can't yet believe. They know something about our potential or needs that we don't yet know. They hold that still secret-to-us vision as a gift. If we are wise, we chance looking deeper within and can recognize that vision and receive that gift. If we claim it, we can go on to offer that gift to the larger world in such a way that the secret is dissolved. We can then affect lives beside us and beyond us in helpful ways.

Here's to saying "yes" to being a holder of visions for others. Here's to saying "yes" to claiming the visions held for us. Here's to saying "yes" to gifting the larger world with who we truly are in all our glorious potential.

Unlimited connections. Unlimited discoveries. Unlimited gifts.

Reflection Questions and Journal Prompts

- *What does this story touch in you?*

- *What are your own stories of being seen, of someone seeing the potential in you or a gift in you, or a need that you have even before you recognized it yourself?*

- *Were you able to claim this need, gift, or potential once it was brought into your awareness? Did this allow you to be able to offer even more of your authentic self in the world?*

- *Do you have stories of being able to see the need, gift or potential in someone else before it was seen by him or her? Was that person able to claim what you saw? How did you experience that individual after this claiming?*

- *How do you think this claiming or dissolving of what may be still secret to us about our needs, gifts, or potential can affect the larger world? What stories might you have about witnessing this?*

Meditation on a Secret Dissolving

Begin by once again finding a place to relax where you won't be disturbed. In this place, allow yourself to take a couple of comfortable deep breaths. On the exhale just allow yourself to release any physical tension that is ready to be released. On the next exhale just allow yourself to release any mental chatter that is ready to be released. Breath by breath and moment by moment, you find yourself relaxing and letting go. Breath by breath, you find yourself softening and opening to whatever is meant to unfold for you in this meditation.

In this relaxed state, you once again allow yourself to travel in your imagination to a place of safety. You may travel to the same place for all meditations or you may travel to different places for each different meditation. Trust your own unique process.

You find yourself now in your safe place. Your senses take in the surrounding environment and you find that each sense is pleased by a perfect match on every level. All that your eyes take in is pleasing. Whatever your sense of smell accesses is just right. The sounds are perfect for you. All is just right for your safe and relaxing experience.

In this safe place, you now can choose to stay and rest and relax right where you are. If this is your choice, you do just that, knowing that it is the right choice for you this day and you select the perfect structure to support you in that experience.

You can also choose to go on a journey that offers an experience of discovery. If this is your choice, you make an inner commitment to the journey knowing that you will be safe all along the way. Having made your commitment, you now notice approaching from the distance is a guide or helper. You feel instantly at ease and trusting of this approaching presence. You know that you are safe and you feel yourself releasing any barriers or fears about this journey of discovery.

As this guide comes right up to you now, you are aware that you feel as though you have known them since the beginning of time. There is an ease and an intimacy that is filled with love and acceptance. This helper begins to guide you along what you have come to understand is a path of discovery. Almost mysteriously, you find your intuition heightened along the way and just by moving along the path you find places here and there where you have additional clarity about your own being. You may find nuggets of clarity about your needs. You may find nuggets of clarity about your gifts and talents. You may find clarity about potentiality and dreams to be realized. Whatever unfolds, the discovery is pleasing and acceptable. You make note of each discovery and give gratitude for it.

Farther along this path of discovery, your helper guides you as the path curves to a different section. Along this section, you may see friends, family or acquaintances. No words are exchanged and they may not even notice your presence. Here, in this place, you are offered an opportunity to consciously deepen your own vision so that you might see with new eyes the needs, gifts, and potential of others. You can consciously intend to heighten your awareness so that you might see what is still secret not only about yourself but also about others. And in this intention, you can also commit to blessing those not-yet-realized gifts and talents whether you are consciously aware of them or just know that they exist. You can intend to live your life in a way that blows on the spark of potentiality. If you say "yes" to this new vision and way of blessing, you may find that your guide gives you a symbol, object or word to help you remember this pledge.

Filled with love, your helper now guides you back to the beginning of the path of discovery. Along the way, you have time to integrate your experience. As you arrive at the beginning you thank your guide and sit to rest a few moments in the safe place where this journey began.

Whether you have been resting in the safe place all along or have been on the path of discovery, you're now ready to bring your conscious awareness back to the place where you were when this meditation began. You take a couple of comfortable deep breaths. You notice the surface that supports you. You notice any sounds or smells in the place where you began your meditation. You are ready to bring your experience back into ordinary consciousness. When you are ready, you open your eyes and take all the time you need to be grounded in your current environment. You take all the time you need to integrate your meditation.

You may wish to share your experience with a friend or companion. You may wish to journal about it.

THE RED SWEATER AND BEING HELD

It all started with a desire for a bit of warm weather in a Midwest winter. We had done the logical sorting of vacation options, but as is often the case for my partner and I, the right trip found us, this time at the checkout counter of a clothing store. Whale watching, here we come. We'd take three planes, our last a four-seater to the Turks and Caicos Islands in the British West Indies. Our particular destination was a small Cay, or island, with minimal tourist options, three lodging choices, one bar/restaurant, and one tiny gift shop attached to the diver's boat shop. We would be living among the locals, and that sounded just right. There would be nine of us, including the tour guide who had taken groups on whale watching trips many times before, though never to this island. We would have plenty of relaxation time, some group activities and, most importantly, we would go out once a day on a skiff and invite the whales to come to us. We were drawn to this particular trip because we felt it was important to honor the whales, not chase them down as many tours groups do.

After months of planning and building excitement, we were ready. Bags, including our new wetsuits, snorkels and fins, were packed; our passports were in hand. Then, the day we were to leave, a large snow event—otherwise known as a major blizzard—was predicted. We decided to stay at a hotel right by the airport the night before our flight to eliminate worry about getting to the airport in the snow. We were covering all our bases. We rose early the next morning and had the shuttle take us across the street to the airport at the earliest possible time. The street was barely passable, the snow heavy, the wind beyond gusting and the cold, oh, it was cold. We barely made it, but we got there and were able to fly out on that first flight of the day. Later, we heard that all subsequent flights were cancelled. We gloated, just a bit, about our good fortune.

Many hours and three plane changes later, we boarded the four-seater to get to our long-awaited island. This was my first small airplane flight and I was thrilled. We flew low, over aqua waters, where coral reefs showed themselves as deeper blue strands that appeared close enough to touch. The pilot was laid back and jovial, and we began to hear our first of many, "no worries." The landing on our destination island was a bit bumpy but heck we were there. The good news was that the two bags were unloaded quickly. The bad news was that neither of those bags was mine. Though it seemed too early to panic, I was already over-heated in my winter attire and knew I needed that suitcase, and fast.

"No worries," the pilot said in his Jamaican-like accent. He would find it and drop it off on his next stop. "Come back to the airport tonight and I'll have it here for you," he said.

"OK, just a minor setback," I thought. Our room, a clean and brightly painted bedroom suite, small sitting area and bathroom, had a front porch that faced the ocean just a few feet away. We could hear the surf and feel the ocean breezes. At the edge of the tide pools, we noticed hammocks swaying in those breezes. This—and the whale sightings—is what we had hoped for. At this moment, a lost suitcase seemed incredibly insignificant.

A bit before seven p.m. we walked to the airport to claim my bag. We could hear the small plane overhead and as we waited for it to land I felt excitement at being able to get out of my warm, Midwest red sweater and into my island attire. The plane landed, bringing two more members of our tour group—and no suitcase for me.

"No worries, ma'am, I will have it here for you first thing tomorrow morning," the pilot promised. "Come back at eight a.m."

"Just a few hours more won't be a big deal," I thought. "I'm sure it will be there next time."

Before bed that evening, our tour guide shared a video about humpbacks. Though we learned many things about these whales, the thing that gave me goose bumps was to learn that the internal structure of the whale's fin looks just like the human hand, complete with "finger" bones. Amazing! We couldn't wait to be with them.

We slept like babies that night, the crisp white sheets and fresh island air lulled me past the anticipation of being reunited with my suitcase in the morning.

We rode a bike borrowed from the villa, that next morning, to get that suitcase. That was fun. What wasn't quite as fun was the fact that the first flight did not bring my suitcase. Another day in my red sweater wasn't appealing, but going out on the skiff for the first time and possibly seeing whales took my mind off my disappointment.

That first time out on the boat brought such excitement, the beginning camaraderie of the group, and the anticipation of a whale encounter. After an hour of enjoying the water, we saw one whale spouting from the distance. The boat stopped and we waited to see if it would approach us, true to the promise not to chase these magnificent creatures. That whale didn't want to be with us. It dove and didn't resurface anywhere we could see it. Still, it was so wonderful to actually see, even from a great distance, a being we had heard so much about. We saw another whale, again from a great distance, which also wanted solitude. After a couple of hours, we returned to shore, happy and fulfilled content for closer encounters on another day.

Still hopeful, we walked once again to the airport for the afternoon flight to find my suitcase.

"No worries," said the pilot.

"No suitcase," I said, disappointed.

There was no clothing store on the island, just that small gift store attached to the dive shop. By this time, the owner felt very sorry for me, so she gave me a free T-shirt and offered to help locate my bag. I nearly fell to the ground in gratitude. A few phone calls later, she told me that my bag was likely flying from island to small island on the plane we took yesterday, which wouldn't necessarily be the plane that came to that island today. She offered to keep working on it. I was to check back before they closed that day. Even without answers, I felt relieved that at least she hadn't said "no worries" and happy that she knew more than I did about how things worked in this corner of the world.

At the end of a full afternoon, we ambled back to the dive shop. The owner told me the good news—she had tracked down my bag (hallelujah)! She also told me the bad news—it wouldn't return to the island until late tomorrow (bummer)! Oh, well, I was making friends with the red sweater, now infused with the scent of suntan lotion, and my new T-shirt. I could wait.

Bringing our snorkels and fins as instructed, we arrived the next morning at our designated meeting spot. Our whole tour climbed aboard the boat and off we went, moving through clear blue waters and warm air to a small deserted island that we could explore. The water off the shore of the island was shallow and the pull of the tide very strong, so we anchored several yards offshore and swam in, more like let ourselves be carried in by that strong tide. This place seemed like something out of a fairy tale. While looking for shells, we noticed that what remained seemed to be only broken bits of shell from the forceful surf. I gave up my search for a whole shell and surrendered to the joy of being there.

Then, as we made our way back to the place where we would swim to the boat, I noticed a whole, beautiful, shiny, white shell. I was thrilled—until I realized that my borrowed wetsuit had no pockets, and the swim back to the boat was going to be very rough. I was about ready to put the shell back on the sand when I decided I would try to carry it inside my wetsuit, over my heart. I wasn't sure if it would remain intact, but I wanted to try it. One by one we entered the water, swam steadily and vigorously against the surf, and made it back to the boat. Only after we were all settled in our seats, did I look inside my wetsuit to discover that the shell was indeed still whole. The symbolism of carrying wholeness near my heart wasn't lost on me. Things were looking up. Perhaps this would be the day that my suitcase would arrive. Hope upon hope!

Back at our bungalow, I was surprised (in a good way) to discover my suitcase right there inside our door. I did the happy dance, and our new friends heard my squeals of delight and came to celebrate with us. They, too, must have been glad to see me in something other than my new T-shirt, borrowed wetsuit and that suntan lotion-scented red sweater.

Day after day passed, and while we had many wonderful experiences, I noticed I was a little sad not to have had any close whale experiences. On our last full day on the island, we were told a storm was predicted and they weren't sure we should even go out on the water. The owner of the dive shop and our boat captain debated and finally the captain said he was willing to give it a go.

"No worries," he said.

I crossed my fingers and climbed aboard. Even if we didn't see any whales, I wanted to say "thank you" to the ocean, to the beings that live in her, and to the whales who had given us so much, even from a distance.

We were tossed and turned, rode the waves up and down, to and fro. We hung on for dear life. The sky was dark, and the clouds seemed to hover only slightly above our heads. Nautical mile after nautical mile, we bounced around. We all gazed intently out to sea, watching, waiting, hoping for one last whale encounter. Time passed, and as we rounded the far side of the island, I think we were all losing hope of a last sighting. I know I was. I surrendered my expectations and tried to settle into the remaining time on the water.

"Look there, starboard side, I think that's a whale spouting!" shouted one woman.

We all turned to look and, sure enough, there she was, diving. Now we had to wait. She could be down a few minutes or a more than half an hour. Until she surfaced again, we wouldn't know if she was staying in the area and, hope upon hope, willing to come closer. Our captain kept glancing up at the darkening sky and did his level best to keep the boat steady as we waited in the choppy sea. We were quiet. I think we were all praying, wishing, or asking for good luck for this last chance.

At once, all of us saw the whale surface just a few yards away from our boat. We watched her with reverence and tears in our eyes. Then, as she got closer and closer, we realized that she was with her calf. Not only were we being honored with a close whale encounter, we had *two* for the hopes of one. In silence, with tears streaming down all our faces, men, women, and captain alike, we watched this mother whale and her calf come right up to our boat.

Then she went *under* our boat and for a moment I think we were all a bit afraid she might tip us. But she did not. Instead, with her calf at her side, she held our boat with her long and graceful fin. For what seemed like a magic-filled eternity, that fin, its structure like the human hand, held us. She held us in our hopes and dreams. She held us in the rough and turbulent seas. She held us in generosity and kindness while sharing her beloved calf and herself with us. No one spoke, and as she and her calf finally swam away we all waved good-bye and continued to weep. In silence, we returned to the physical place where we had begun our journey, yet so not where we started.

The abundance of this trip was awe-inspiring. Lessons of "no worries," of surrendering both suitcases and expectations were given. Lessons of carrying wholeness right next to the heart were taken in. The gifts of, and connections with, former strangers, human and cetacean alike, were received. Being willing to move through the storm and then be open to wishes and dreams being fulfilled was taught and learned. And the experience beyond words, of being held—literally *held*—by something magical, mysterious and larger than ourselves, was embraced in awe.

I still have that red sweater. I don't wear it anymore, but sometimes I get it out of my closet, hold it close to my heart and take in the scent of tropical air, of friendship and connection, of surrender and wholeness, of magic and being held, and yes, the fragrance of not-yet-faded suntan lotion.

Reflection Questions and Journal Prompts

- *What, if anything, speaks to you in this story?*

- *Tell about a time where your intuition guided you.*

- *Does the metaphor of carrying wholeness next to your heart resonate in any way for you? If so, what are those stories?*

- *What are your stories of symbolically moving through storms, releasing expectations, and yet being willing to have your dreams and wishes come true?*

- *What are your stories of being held by something larger than yourself, something mysterious, something magical?*

- *Do you have any stories of "no worries"?*

Suggested Activities or Experiences

- *The next trip or outing you plan, if you don't already, try centering and letting your intuition guide you. This could be a large trip or even just a few-minute outing.*

- *Maybe you are called to carry a symbol of your wholeness next to your heart. What might that symbol be for you?*

- *Perhaps there is a drawing, painting, sculpture or dance for you that is about letting go of expectations and being open to wishes and dreams coming true.*

- *You might take a few quiet moments each morning to imagine being held by something larger than yourself, something magical and mysterious. You might enjoy this so much that you pause several times during your day to repeatedly imagine that very thing.*

Meditation on Being Held

Begin by finding a comfortable place to sit or lie down where you won't be disturbed. Allow your awareness to come to your breath. For now, just notice the breath. In and out, in and out. Let the breath breathe you. Be breathed by the breath. Take all the time you need right now to just be with the breath.

And when you are ready, you welcome your body into this day, into this experience. Begin by bringing loving awareness to the body. Just notice how the body is at this moment of this day. There is no need to change anything and there is no judgment, only loving awareness of the body. Notice any places of tension, discomfort or holding. Notice any places of ease, flow and comfort in the body. Welcome the body into this experience, this day and breathe a breath of acceptance to the body. Only after extending awareness, welcome and acceptance to the body do you notice if there is any tension, holding or energy in the body, that is no longer needed, that is ready to be released. If so, then you just let it go, perhaps sailing it out on the exhaled breath. And if this created any new spaciousness in the body, you can use your breath to expand out the health and wholeness that lives at your core into this newly opened space. You may also wish to partner that with breathing in the wholeness energy available in the larger universe outside of you. Breathing in, and expanding out health and wholeness for the body.

You can extend this same welcome to the emotion self. Begin by noticing with loving awareness whatever emotions are present with you this moment of this day. No judgment, no right or wrong, no need to change anything. For now just notice the emotion self. Welcome the emotion self into this day. When you are ready, breathe a breath of acceptance to the emotion self no matter what is found there. And only after this welcoming and this extending of acceptance do you notice if there is any emotion energy that is no longer needed that is ready to be released. And if there is, you just let it go. No force, no effort, just releasing. Perhaps you send it out with the support of the exhaled breath. Release it in whatever is your way. And if this has created any new spaciousness in your emotion self you expand out the emotional health and wholeness that lives at your core into this newly opened space. You may also wish to partner this with breathing in the larger

emotion health and wholeness energy available from the larger universe outside of you. Breathe in and expand out to fill the emotion self with health and wholeness.

You can give this same gift now to your thinking mind. Taking time to pause and notice with loving awareness the thoughts and beliefs moving through the mind along with noticing any mental chatter present at this moment of this day. Pausing to notice the thoughts without the need to engage them and perhaps remembering that the thoughts are not necessarily your deeper truths. After a few moments of noticing you welcome your thinking mind into this day and this experience. Breathe a breath of acceptance to your mind. And only after noticing, welcoming and extending acceptance do you notice if there are any old beliefs that are no longer true for you or any mental chatter or thoughts that are no longer needed. If there are, and they are ready to be released, you just let them go. Perhaps with the support of your exhaled breath or whatever is your way. And if this creates any new spaciousness in your mind, you expand out the peace and wholeness that live at your core to fill this space. Again, you may wish to partner this with the peace and harmony that also lives in the world outside of you. Breathing in and expanding out peace and harmony for the mind.

Now you have created an environment where your wisest Self can emerge. And so you pause and breathe and be as this Self that is your true nature. You take all the time you need deepening your connection as this wise and expansive Self.

You may now choose to stay, breathe and relax in the current environment that you have created or you may choose to take a journey of being held. You trust and honor whatever decision you make.

If you are choosing a journey of being held, you now see in your mind's eye a path that wends its way through a pleasing environment. You journey on this path in a way that is pleasant and safe for you. You trust that you have all that you need to make this journey.

When the time is right, you instinctively find yourself in a setting that is the perfect place in which to be held. You notice how the sounds, smells, temperature and sights are all pleasing to your senses. You also notice that residing in this environment is the perfect holder for you. You approach your perfect holder, be it a person, a guide, an animal, an inanimate object or something else. In a way that is just right for you, your holder welcomes you and you feel embraced by this holding. Perhaps you find that it is your infant self that is held. Perhaps you find that it is your older child self that is held, your adolescent self or a more adult self. Whatever part of you appears in this holding you trust that it is just right. You allow this self to really release into the safety of this holding. You surrender yourself to this holding by something larger than yourself, perhaps something magical. You find yourself being held in generosity and kindness. You find yourself being held in safety. You find yourself held in a way that would be comforting in turbulent times or in easy, smooth times. You find yourself held in unconditional love that is spacious enough to allow for differences.

Just notice how you respond to this holding. There is no right or wrong, only your own way of being held. You stay in this place and way of being held for as long as feels just right for you. When the time of this holding feels complete you know that you can return to this holding at any time in the future. Before leaving to return the way you have come, you give gratitude for this experience and bring with you a word, symbol or felt sense to remind you of being held by something larger than yourself.

You return now, at your own perfect pace, retracing the way you have come. When you arrive back where you began this journey of being held, you take a few deep breaths and begin to bring your awareness back, further still, to the beginning environment in which you began this whole meditation. You reacquaint yourself with the sounds of the place where you began and the temperature of the place where you began. And when you are ready you open your eyes, take a couple more deep breaths and find yourself back in this present moment.

You may wish to journal about your experience of being held or share with a trusted friend or companion.

THE LAP OF THE MOTHER

When one's spirituality is based in nature everything in the natural world is holy, is sacred, and brings us the experience of the Everywhere Presence. Many indigenous cultures, the Wiccan tradition and Celtic spirituality connect faith and the natural world. So does Claudia.

One day, Claudia was driving home after a long day of work. She was the kind of tired that one good night's sleep won't erase. The busyness and stresses of her life had gradually distanced her from her spiritual needs and she pondered what she might do about this. The tension in her face relaxed as she anticipated a rare, free evening at home in her favorite fall season. Then what she saw on the side of the road removed her quickly from this reflective place. A raccoon lay still, motionless, most likely hit by a car.

Claudia's inner debate began. One voice said, "Just keep going. The raccoon is probably dead and there's nothing you can do anyway. It's been a long time since you could just enjoy an evening at home in this kind of weather."

Another voice had a different message, "Dead or alive, that raccoon matters. You can't just drive by as if it is nothing, means nothing. The life of that animal, as much as your life, holds meaning. You have to go back. And besides, perhaps it is still alive and you can do something to aid its suffering."

Claudia circled the block, pulled over to the side of the street, and got out, walked to the body of the raccoon. She bent down and watched for signs of breathing. There were none. She reached out and felt its body—still warm but cooling. Knowing now that it was dead, though not long dead, she knew the physical suffering had ended. She could have gone back to her truck and just driven away. Or could she? She did go back to her truck, but instead of getting behind the wheel, she dug around in the back and found a mechanic's cloth, the kind you lay on to change your oil or get a glimpse of something under the vehicle. The cloth was rumpled and stained but it was all she had.

She carried it back to the lifeless raccoon and laid the cloth on the asphalt. With reverence, she bent down, lifted the raccoon's body, and laid it in the center of the cloth. She gathered up each corner of the cloth laying it over the body. Then she lifted up the swaddling bundle and carried it gently back to her truck. Pausing for a few quiet breaths, she connected with her inner knowing of what to do and where to go next.

Driving toward home, Claudia was struck by the clarity with which she acted. Later, she would scoff at the idea of her being a hero or of acting above and beyond. She would say that she was simply following a strong inner voice of guidance that surprised even her. But that inner sense of direction led her to park close to the river near her home. For some time, the busyness of life had kept her from walking along that river, from visiting what she calls "The Mother Tree."

Years ago, she'd come upon a tree along the river that seemed to have a strong, maternal presence. At her base, her roots formed a lap of sorts that spoke of holding and comfort. Claudia had visited this tree often in her own times of confusion and challenge and had found great comfort sitting with this Mother Tree, had found it to be a place where she could feel the Presence of something larger than herself.

Now, Claudia gathered up the raccoon bundle and began the trek to the river. She then traveled along the river, feeling as if she were acting in some way outside of herself, outside of ordinary consciousness. She felt protective of the raccoon and felt tenderness and compassion about the suffering and ending of a life.

She walked in solitude until she reached the Mother Tree. There, with only the autumn breezes as her witness, she laid the raccoon's body in the Mother's lap.

She remembers saying a prayer of gratitude for the life of the raccoon, of blessing it, and of releasing it to the Earth Mother. She didn't know where the words came from that she spoke aloud in a whispered voice, she just knew that they came easily and without effort.

After a time of quiet she retraced her steps back along the riverbank to her truck, then to home.

Claudia's life is still busy. She can easily recite her list of stresses. She acknowledges that she isn't perfect at tending her spiritual needs. But, sometimes when Claudia feels most overwhelmed and mired in the details of life, she accesses the memory of this story. It is then that she feels her tension dissolve a bit, feels her heart open and her breathing deepen, and notices her perspective shifting beyond the detail-absorbed mouse's view to the soaring, expansive view of the eagle. It is here that she finds herself held in comfort. It is here that she lies in the "lap of the mother."

Reflection Questions and Journal Prompts

- *What, if anything, speaks to you in this story?*

- *Are there times when you "run over" yourself? Are there times when you ignore that which is important or life sustaining? If you reflect back, what is going on then: feeling like you don't have time, worrying about what others will think, rejecting the call to something that doesn't seem logical, something else?*

- *Have you found yourself run over by others who are unaware, unconscious, or perhaps even intentional in the running over of you? How do you respond? Do you desire a shift in this response?*

- *Have there been times when you have, consciously or unconsciously, run over others? What was happening in your life then? Have you found a need to make amends? Forgive yourself?*

- *Are there places for you of releasing, healing and blessing, like the Mother Tree?*

- *How might your life be different if you stopped running over yourself? How might your life be different if you stopped and tended your wounded self with kindness, compassion and reverence?*

- *How would our world be different if we tended all beings this way? Can you imagine us all being the Lap of the Mother for each other and ourselves? Is there one simple way you could be that for yourself or someone else today?*

Suggested Activities or Experiences

- *Once you imagine what your Mother Tree might be like, you might sculpt her. You might draw or paint her. You might put on some special music and dance as her. You might go out and find her in nature. You might write or create a poem about her.*

- *You might take a day and imagine being held in the lap of your Mother Tree all day. Just notice what that day is like for you.*

- *You might take a day and imagine that everyone you meet is being held in the lap of his or her own Mother Tree that day. What is that day like for you?*

- *You might imagine a day where everyone and everything is held in the lap of the Mother Tree of his or her choice. What is that day like for you?*

Meditation of the Mother Tree

Begin by finding a comfortable place to sit or lie down where you won't be disturbed. Close your eyes if that is comfortable for you. Allow your awareness to come to your breath. For now, just notice the breath. In and out, in and out. Let the breath breathe you. Be breathed by the breath. Take all the time you need right now to just be with the breath.

When you are ready, you welcome your body into this day, into this experience. Begin by bringing loving awareness to the body. Just notice the body and how it is at this moment of this day. There is no need to change anything and there is no judgment, only loving awareness of the body. Notice any places of tension, discomfort or holding. Notice any places of ease, flow and comfort in the body. Welcome the body into this experience, this day and breathe a breath of acceptance to the body. Only after extending awareness, welcome and acceptance to the body do you notice if there is any tension, holding or energy in the body, that is no longer needed, that is ready to be released. If so, then you just let it go, perhaps sailing it out on the exhaled breath. And if this created any new spaciousness in the body, you can use your breath to expand out the health and wholeness that lives at your core into this newly opened space. You may also wish to partner that with breathing in the wholeness energy available in the larger universe outside of you. Breathing in, and expanding out health and wholeness for the body.

You can extend this same welcome to the emotion self. Begin by noticing with loving awareness whatever emotions are present with you this moment of this day. No judgment, no right or wrong, no need to change anything. For now just notice the emotion self. Welcome the emotion self into this day. When you are ready, breathe a breath of acceptance to the emotion self no matter what is found there. And only after this welcoming and this extending of acceptance, do you notice if there is any emotion energy that is no longer needed that is ready to be released. If there is, you just let it go. No force, no effort, just release. Perhaps you send it out with the support of the exhaled breath. Release it in whatever way feels right to you. And if this has created any new spaciousness in your emotion self, you expand out the emotional health and wholeness that lives at your core into this newly opened space. You may also wish to partner this with breathing in the larger emotion health and wholeness energy available from the larger universe outside of you. Breathe in and expand out to fill the emotion self with health and wholeness.

You can give this same gift now to your thinking mind. Take time to pause and notice with loving awareness the thoughts and beliefs moving through the mind along with any mental chatter present at this moment of this day. Pause to notice the thoughts without the need to engage them and perhaps remember that the thoughts are not necessarily your deeper truths. After a few moments, you welcome your thinking mind into this day and this experience. Breathe a breath of acceptance to your mind. And only after noticing, welcoming and extending acceptance do you notice if there are any old beliefs that are no longer true for you or any mental chatter or thoughts that are no longer needed. If there are, and they are ready to be released, just let them go. Perhaps with the support of your exhaled breath or whatever is your way. And if this creates any new spaciousness in your mind, you expand out the peace and wholeness that lives at your core to fill this space. Again, you may wish to partner this with the peace and harmony that also lives in the world outside of you. Breathing in and expanding out peace and harmony for the mind.

Now you have created an environment where your wisest Self can emerge. And so you pause and breathe and be as this Self that is your true nature. You take all the time you need deepening your connection as this wise and expansive Self.

You can rest here and enjoy this as your complete mediation. Or you can choose to go on your own journey to the "Mother Tree."

If you are choosing to journey, make an inner commitment and agreement to explore.

Imagine that you are in a wonderful place in nature where there are many beautiful trees of all kinds. You see a path wending through the trees and you decide to take it. You may be traveling by yourself or you may have the company of a guide or companion. Trust yourself to know what is just right for you.

Along the path you come upon a part of yourself that may be wounded in some way, troubled, worried or struggling with something or someone. You pause and allow yourself to lovingly tend to this part of you. Trust yourself to know whatever is called for and what will provide the most love and support to this part of you. If there are special supplies or materials that would offer tending, they are magically available.

35

When and if it feels right to you, you tenderly pick up and carry this part of yourself to your nearby Mother Tree. This tree exudes love, compassion and empathy. This tree radiates light and unconditional acceptance. At its base, this tree's roots form a bowl or lap that can hold whatever needs to be held. When it is the perfect time, you gently and with much love, lay the suffering part of yourself down in that place of immense love. Perhaps you even merge with this Mother Tree in offering love and comfort to that wounded self.

When the wounded self is ready, she may merge with you and return to the trailhead where the path began. She may ask that you carry her in her tended form back to the beginning. It may be that the Mother Tree and you are the same and you all merge together and return back to the start of the path. It could be that something entirely different happens. Trust your own unfolding here and know that whatever happens, it is the highest and most loving good.

Arriving at the beginning of the path now, you turn around and give gratitude for the journey. With whatever has transpired, you begin to return now to ordinary consciousness. Notice the surface of the structure that supported your body from the beginning of this meditation. Notice any sounds in that environment. Notice the temperature on your skin. Allow yourself a couple of comfortably deep breaths. When you are ready, open your eyes and allow yourself all the time you need to reorient to your present awareness.

You may wish to journal or share your experience with a friend or companion.

LADY ELEPHANT RIDER

As a clinical social worker, I've had the opportunity to meet many memorable people in my profession. One of them was a nine-year-old girl named Tish. She functioned below the norm intellectually, and so in terms of book smarts and some reasoning, Tish lacked certain finesse. Her thinking was very concrete. If you forgot how literal she was, her responses or comments would quickly remind you.

What Tish lacked in her powers of abstract reasoning and intelligence, however, she made up for in her refreshing and matter-of-fact approach to life. She also loved to gently tease and laugh. Often Tish's jokes made sense only to her, and yet I was always drawn into the laughter because of the vigor with which she told her stories. She was a delight, no question about it. Oh, sometimes she was incredibly stubborn and yet that quality of not giving in often translated into persistence at times when I seemed to have more trouble accepting her life circumstances than did she. She kept her heels dug in and waited out whatever might seem like another unkind hand dealt by fate. I was glad for the strength of these qualities in her as she moved toward being separated from foster parents who were no longer able to care for her.

During one of our sessions, Tish chose to play a game that requires players to take turns answering questions from randomly selected cards. I've played this game with kids for years and never cease to be amazed at how much information it elicits from a person, both about herself and about the other players. Tish and I answered questions such as, "Tell about your ideal life," or "The best thing about today is . . ." and as we did, I stored away tidbits of new information that might be of help in my later work with her. One of her questions was, "Tell about something you do which requires that you use all of you . . . your mind, body, heart and soul." Tish's answer—math! I'm sure for Tish that was very true. School was not easy for her and she worked very hard to get passing grades. How aptly put and how clearly she communicated her determination to succeed with just one word.

We answered still more questions, deepening our knowledge of each other. The question "If you could be famous, what would you like to be known for?" was directed at me, so I began sorting through various possibilities aloud.

"Well," I said, "maybe a singer or writer or someone who helps people."

"Or, a lady elephant rider," said Tish.

I raised an eyebrow until I saw a serious look on her face, a look that seemed to accompany a true desire to help me make my final answer. I lowered the eyebrow. The idea of me—someone who is clearly not dainty and has only minimal coordination—becoming an elephant rider was a purely unexpected curve ball from nowhere. I began to shake with laughter at the mental image. Soon, Tish joined me in laughter. We laughed until we cried and our sides hurt. When at last we could continue our game, Tish's next question was, "Name two famous people you'd like to have for parents."

In all seriousness, she replied, "A clown and an elephant rider."

Now I was beginning to catch on. This kid had been to a circus. This kid's frame of reference was definitely a circus! Slowly our eyes connected and again we began to laugh and laugh some more.

"You are a delight," I said to her.

"I know it," she said.

I hope Tish still knows what a delight she is. She taught me many things during our time together. I learned how to step out of the ordinary, how to appreciate life's simplicity, the joys of unconventionality, and unexpected things. Now, when life seems overwhelming or I'm too full of myself, all I have to do is picture my career as a lady elephant rider and suddenly everything is back in perspective. I don't know where Tish is today, but I hope that wherever she is, she knows that I have never forgotten her. After all, elephants never forget—and neither do lady elephant riders.

Reflection Questions and Journal Prompts

- *What draws your attention in this story?*

- *Can you speak to times where digging in your heels and waiting served you in some way?*

- *What in your life has required that you use all of you—mind, body, heart and soul?*

- *Like Tish's circus experience, how does your frame of reference color your current perspective? Has this narrowed your life, made it more expansive, or some of each? How?*

- *Can you tell about a time you stepped out of your ordinary perspective and experienced the unexpected?*

- *In the Hindu tradition, there is a god named Ganesha that has the body of a man and the head of an elephant. It is believed that Ganesha uses his trunk to sweep the path clear and is known to remove obstacles. People in this tradition call upon Ganesha for assistance in removing obstacles in their life. Tish found some ways of coping that helped her remove obstacles. As a lady elephant rider, I have learned to call upon Ganesha for this same gift. Can you share about any places in your life that you might call upon the energy of removing obstacles?*

- *What do you know to be true about yourself and hope always to remember?*

Suggested Activities or Experiences

Sculpt, draw, write a poem or song, and/or put on some music and move to it as a way of expressing yourself as a "delight."

Meditation on Removing Obstacles

Begin by finding a comfortable place to sit or lie down where you won't be disturbed. Allow your awareness to come to your breath. For now, just notice the breath. In and out, in and out. Just breathe. Let the breath breathe you. Be breathed by the breath. Take all the time you need right now to just be with the breath.

And when you are ready, you welcome your body into this moment, into this experience. Begin by bringing loving awareness to the body. Just notice the body and how it is at this moment, of this day. There is no need to change anything and there is no judgment, only loving awareness of the body. Notice any places of tension, discomfort or holding. Notice any places of ease, flow and comfort in the body. Welcome the body into this experience, this day and breathe a breath of acceptance to the body. Only after extending awareness, welcome and acceptance to the body do you notice if there is any tension, holding or energy in the body, that is no longer needed, that is ready to be released. If so, then you just let it go, perhaps sailing it out on the exhaled breath. And if this created any new spaciousness in the body you can use your breath to expand out the health and wholeness that lives at your core into this newly opened space. You may also wish to partner that with breathing in the wholeness energy available in the larger universe outside of you. Breathing in, and expanding out health and wholeness for the body.

You can extend this same welcome to the emotion self. Begin by noticing with loving awareness whatever emotions are present with you this moment of this day. No judgment, no right or wrong, no need to change anything. For now just notice the emotion self. Welcome the emotion self into this day. When you are ready, breathe a breath of acceptance to the emotion self no matter what is found there. And only after this welcoming and this extending of acceptance do you notice if there is any emotion energy that is no longer needed that is ready to be released. And if there is you just let it go. No force, no effort, just release. Perhaps you send it out with the support of the exhaled breath. Release it in whatever is your way. And if this has created any new spaciousness in your emotion self, you expand out the emotional health and wholeness that lives at your core into this newly opened space. You may also wish to partner this with breathing in the larger

emotion health and wholeness energy available from the larger universe outside of you. Breathe in and expand out to fill the emotion self with health and wholeness.

You can give this same gift now to your thinking mind. Taking time to pause and notice with loving awareness the thoughts and beliefs moving through the mind along with noticing any mental chatter present at this moment of this day. Pausing to notice the thoughts without the need to engage them and perhaps remembering that the thoughts are not necessarily your deeper truths. After a few moments of noticing you welcome your thinking mind into this day and this experience. Breathe a breath of acceptance to your mind. And only after noticing, welcoming and extending acceptance do you notice if there are any old beliefs that are no longer true for you or any mental chatter or thoughts that are no longer needed. If there are, and they are ready to be released, you just let them go. Perhaps with the support of your exhaled breath or whatever is your way. And if this creates any new spaciousness in your mind, you expand out the peace and wholeness that lives at your core to fill this space. Again, you may wish to partner this with the peace and harmony that also lives in the world outside of you. Breathing in and expanding out peace and harmony for the mind.

Now you have created an environment where your wisest Self can emerge. And so you pause and breathe and be as this Self that is your true nature. You take all the time you need deepening your connection as this wise and expansive Self.

You may now choose to remain in this place breathing and relaxing for the remainder of this meditation time. Or, you may choose to explore a journey of removing obstacles.

If you choose to journey further, you allow yourself, in your own pace and time, to arrive at a safe place in nature. This is a place that is pleasant for all your senses. In this place your feel that you are free to more deeply explore. Perhaps at this point you notice a path that you wish to follow. Perhaps you notice that you are called to explore where there is no clear path. Just notice what it is that draws you.

Before setting out on this exploration, if it feels right to you, you call upon the energy of Ganesha, or the more general energy of having your path cleared for you.

Then you begin to explore. Perhaps you notice that the way is magically clear. Perhaps you notice Ganesha clearing the path for you with his trunk. Perhaps you notice another guide or helper clearing for you. Perhaps you notice another version of yourself that clears the way. Just notice.

Just notice what is being cleared. You may find some struggle places in your life arising for clearing. You may find a more general sense of your life path being clear. Just notice. Notice whatever gifts of this journey are being presented for you. Perhaps you notice a shift in perspective. Perhaps you notice the removal of old beliefs that have contributed to a sense of stuckness. Perhaps old ways of seeing yourself are loosened. Perhaps you see more clearly the authentic you. Perhaps you notice a sense of lightness. There is no right or wrong. Just notice what your own journey brings.

When you have received all that was meant for you in this journey, you return with gratitude to the place where you began this exploration. As you arrive at the beginning place in nature, you pause to take a few breaths and deeply anchor any gifts from this experience that you wish to take with you into your life.

When you are ready you allow your conscious awareness to return to the environment where you first began this meditation. You notice the surface that is supporting your body. You notice the sounds. You take a couple of deep breaths and then allow your eyes to open. You take all the time you need to return to waking, alert, consciousness.

You may wish to journal about your experience or share with a trusted friend or companion.

BECOMING STILL

This is a fast world. We used to measure that by microwave and convection ovens and by fast food restaurants with drive-through windows. Instant oatmeal has been bypassed by instant messaging. The regular old internet bypassed by hi-speed internet. We hurry faster and faster and try to do more and more and feel stress building and building. I know that after years of practicing the art of slowing down, becoming still and encouraging my clients to do the same, after re-learning the relaxation response in my body, the hurrying can creep in, can overtake me with its sneaky promise of accomplishing more so that I might find rest at the end of a very long list. When I buy into that rationale, that false sense of urgency, even for a second, I feel that inner hurrying sensation as my jaw tenses, my heart speeds up, my muscles tighten and the old thinking returns.

There isn't enough time but you can do it if you hurry. We have to get there by the appointed time. Early is better.

I walk faster, drive faster; feel more impatient and irritated with things and people that are just minding their own business. Nose to the grindstone, I rush and hurry and stress until something, someone, or someplace reminds me to come home; home to myself and the deep river of peace that flows under all this craziness. Home to what really matters and to the opportunity to experience life rather than analyze it, observe it or be numb and unconscious to it. This place of "home" is the place where we can gather the fullness of the gifts available and hear the inner whispers of the soul.

Over-stimulating, loud music-blaring, lights-flashing, game-crowded pizza places with mascots to celebrate children on their birthdays didn't seem like a place where I would remember the stillness of coming home. But there it was.

The love of a six-year-old can get me to many places. Being invited to attend the big birthday celebration for Sammy was an honor that touched my heart. Morgan and I arrived at this place of birthday chaos in time to meet Sammy, his younger brother, Colin, and their parents in the full parking lot. The closer we moved to the entrance the louder the music became. Walking through the door felt like a full attack on every sense. The heavy smell of pizza mingled with sugar. The place was hot and packed. Game after noisy game filled three large rooms. So many people and though these were families with squealing and crying children, I was reminded of my college day concerts. The volume certainly equaled those rowdy musical performances. A yellow pall emanated from the game lights and we all looked like we had arrived from another planet. Inside we were joined by some of Sammy's friends.

We found the reserved table where we dropped off our gifts and shed our coats. We joined the kids in playing a variety of games. Some games spit out random ticket stubs that the kids went wild over since they could save them for later redemption at the Wall of Prizes. The Wall of Prizes offered plastic green fangs, cheap cardboard toys and other junk that seemed like valuable gems to the kids. Dazed and ready to sit down way before they were, we were still grateful to be sharing this time with them.

A young female employee came around announcing in a loud voice that the mascot, that the children seemed to revere, would soon be arriving. There were screams and cheers and everyone scrambled to their reserved tables, at which I might add, we were packed like sardines. The pizza arrived and we ate and drank while waiting excitedly for the birthday mascot.

Soon and with much fanfare, the birthday mascot arrived. He shook the hand of each boy and girl identified by the birthday crowns they wore. He gave each Olympic-birthday-child a medallion to wear around their neck. He had them up dancing and sitting in his lap. They hugged and snuggled with him in a rapture I thought was only reserved for Santa Claus.

After the mascot left, each child feeling special and richly celebrated, things began to wind down. But, wait . . . there was more. One last big ritual awaited Sammy. We walked with Sammy and his parents to, what I now call, the Tornado Tube, a large, clear, Plexiglas cylinder. Sammy enters the tube and the staff person shuts the door. She asks if Sammy is ready. He nods his head yes. Flipping the "on" switch results in the most ferocious blast of continuous blowing air that I have ever witnessed. From the floor, hundreds of those prized ticket stubs now rise and fly with great velocity in the air all around Sammy. It reminds me of the debris caught by tornados. During the first few moments, Sammy frantically flails his arms and tries to grasp some of the coveted tickets, to no avail, they are moving faster than the speed of light. I notice that I am worried that this will be a depressing end to a celebratory day.

Then, something remarkable happens. Sammy slowly brings his arms first to his sides and then, hands palm down, holds them in front of his waist. Still. He holds them completely still. There is no frantic striving now. The tickets gather themselves by the dozens into his tiny, stationary hands. They come effortlessly to him. The stillness brings the tickets to him and he is smiling.

I find myself tearing up, in awe that here, in this place of birthday chaos, I find a reminder about the power of stillness. I am taught once again, by a six-year-old this time, how all the striving, frantic, hurried, needy grasping does not bring gifts to us. I am re-taught that the gifts will find us if we but become still. Sammy found a way to come home on his birthday and receive the prizes that brings—and I received a surprise gift at the same time.

Now when I find myself hurrying, moving away from the home deep within me, all I have to do is remember the Tornado Tube, Sammy's wisdom, and becoming still.

Reflections and Journal Prompts

- *What, if anything, touches you about this story?*

- *Have you noticed the busy, fast-paced world affecting you? If so, what happens in your body, mind, emotions and spirit as a result?*

- *Have you had gifts of remembering something important to your health and wholeness coming from unexpected places or people? If so, what are those stories?*

- *What helps you remember your home, the place where peace and stillness lives deep within? What is most important to you when you are home? When you come home what changes in your body, mind, emotion and spirit?*

- *How does this getting still affect your life? What gifts are there for you in the stillness?*

Suggested Activities or Experiences

- *You may wish to enter your day intentionally looking for unexpected reminders of what's truly important to you.*

- *The next time you find yourself in a place or situation that can potentially take you away from your inner home, you might watch with new eyes to find an unexpected gift or blessing.*

- *You might send a note of thanks to someone who has helped you remember something you value.*

- *You might try standing and allow your arms to flail about as if trying to grasp at all that you wish to have in your life. Then try bringing your arms to your sides, placing your fingers together, your palms face down in front of your waist and becoming still. Pause in this posture, breathing deeply for several moments. Just notice how this is for you.*

Meditation on Becoming Still

Begin by finding a comfortable place to sit or lie down where you won't be disturbed. Allow your awareness to come to your breath. For now, just notice the breath. In and out, in and out. Just breathe. Let the breath breathe you. Be breathed by the breath. Take all the time you need right now to just be with the breath.

And when you are ready, you welcome your body into this moment, into this experience. Begin by bringing loving awareness to the body. Just notice the body and how it is at this moment, of this day. There is no need to change anything and there is no judgment, only loving awareness of the body. Notice any places of tension, discomfort or holding. Notice any places of ease, flow and comfort in the body. Welcome the body into this experience, this day and breathe a breath of acceptance to the body. Only after extending awareness, welcome and acceptance to the body do you notice if there is any tension, holding or energy in the body, that is no longer needed, that is ready to be released. If so, then you just let it go, perhaps sailing it out on the exhaled breath. And if this created any new spaciousness in the body, you can use your breath to expand out the health and wholeness that lives at your core into this newly opened space. You may also wish to partner that with breathing in the wholeness energy available in the larger universe outside of you. Breathing in, and expanding out health and wholeness for the body.

You can extend this same welcome to the emotion self. Begin by noticing with loving awareness whatever emotions are present with you this moment of this day. No judgment, no right or wrong, no need to change anything. For now just notice the emotion self. Welcome the emotion self into this day. When you are ready, breathe a breath of acceptance to the emotion self no matter what is found there. And only after this welcoming and this extending of acceptance do you notice if there is any emotion energy that is no longer needed that is ready to be released. And if there is, you just let it go. No force, no effort, just release. Perhaps you send it out with the support of the exhaled breath. Release it in whatever is your way. And if this has created any new spaciousness in your emotion self, you expand out the emotional health and wholeness that lives at your core into this newly opened space. You may also wish to partner this with breathing in the larger

emotion health and wholeness energy available from the larger universe outside of you. Breathe in and expand out to fill the emotion self with health and wholeness.

You can give this same gift now to your thinking mind. Taking time to pause and notice with loving awareness the thoughts and beliefs moving through the mind along with noticing any mental chatter present at this moment of this day. Pausing to notice the thoughts without the need to engage them and perhaps remembering that the thoughts are not necessarily your deeper truths. After a few moments of noticing you welcome your thinking mind into this day and this experience. Breathe a breath of acceptance to your mind. And only after noticing, welcoming and extending acceptance do you notice if there are any old beliefs that are no longer true for you or any mental chatter or thoughts that are no longer needed. If there are, and they are ready to be released, you just let them go. Perhaps with the support of your exhaled breath or whatever is your way. And if this creates any new spaciousness in your mind, you expand out the peace and wholeness that lives at your core to fill this space. Again, you may wish to partner this with the peace and harmony that also lives in the world outside of you. Breathing in and expanding out peace and harmony for the mind.

Now you have created an environment where your wisest Self can emerge. And so you pause and breathe and be as this Self that is your true nature. You take all the time you need deepening your connection as this wise and expansive Self.

You can choose to stay in this place of connection with your expansive Self. You might also choose to go on a journey of becoming still.

If you choose to go on a journey of becoming still, you find yourself in a place or situation where there is some type chaos or challenge to becoming still. You might even imagine yourself in the "Tornado Tube." Initially, you might notice that this place or situation attempts to pull you out of your center and into the chaos. You are aware of your body, mind, emotion and spirit's response. You might handle this circumstance by stilling first your body. Perhaps you even bring your arms to your sides and your hands, palms down, to the front of your body, like Sammy in the story, pausing in stillness. Perhaps you intentionally slow your breathing. Notice how you find a response that doesn't armor you against the chaos but rather shifts something inside of you so that you can be still amidst the chaos. Notice what gifts you harvest as a result. Notice how you are able to come back home to your center, to your place of peace.

You now anchor this experience deep inside, in your own way and time, so that you can take it out into the world in real and practical ways. Perhaps there is a symbol, an image, a movement, or a tangible object that helps you in this anchoring.

When you are ready, you begin to return your awareness to the place where you first began this meditation. You feel your body supported, take a couple of deep breaths, and open your eyes when it is the right time for you.

You may wish to journal about your experience of becoming still or share with a trusted friend or companion.

THE CRYSTAL BOWL

There are many ways to view the human self. What many of these views share is the belief that we are complex aspects of the whole. Imagine a large circle divided into equal pie-shaped sections. This drawing, on a handout from a psychotherapy class in my graduate program, is a clear memory. We were to write a descriptor of ourselves such as "happy" in each "slice." Then, in the opposite slice, we were to write its opposite, for example, "sad." The message was that our wholeness (the circle) contains many seemingly opposite qualities of the self.

In psychosynthesis, another perspective, it is believed that we have a transpersonal self and an ego or personality part of the self. The personality part of the self can be further divided into subparts, such as inner critic, wounded child, perfectionist, and worrier, for example. We hear the transpersonal self referred to by such names as High Self, Bigger Picture Self, Buddha Nature, Large Mind, Spirit, Soul, Christ Light, Higher Consciousness Self, Wisdom Self, and so forth.

A Jungian therapist, Seena Frost, developed another way of seeing ourselves called SoulCollage®, which uses visual art to work with the one self and the many selves that comprise the whole.

≈

Many of my clients have struggled to integrate all aspects of themselves, here is a story of a remarkable way in which integration of our many selves unfolded.

Mary is an amazingly intelligent and creative woman who had excelled in her chosen profession before retirement. She pondered life's biggest questions and had seen many therapists, doctors, ministers and spiritual directors over the years to work on these issues and deal with her depression. In one of our earliest sessions, Mary gave voice to some frustration. "I have worked on understanding my inner child, my inner adolescent, my depressed self, my married self, my mother self, my professional self and my angry self and on and on," she said. "I still struggle, I still feel fragmented. How do I pull all this together?"

It was clear Mary had lived out a commitment to her healing and had done a great deal in that regard. I affirmed her for her dedication to her healing and said that I wanted to brainstorm ways of integrating all that she had done. It was clear to me that Mary, like most of us raised in the Western World, tried to change things by changing her thinking. While she had some success with this emphasis in her previous therapy, it seemed incomplete. I asked her to ponder approaching this integration in a different way. In spite of a mysterious quality to what we were exploring, Mary was willing. So, we pondered, we brainstormed and we explored possibilities.

Mary and I spoke of ritual and ceremony as a way to help us "get" things on a deeper level of our consciousness, to help with deeper healing. I shared with her some of my favorite books on the topic of healing ritual. Time after time, I encouraged Mary to trust her own wisdom to know what ritual, ceremony or other way of integration spoke to her deepest self.

One day, Mary came into my office for a session carrying a large canvas bag obviously filled with something. She said she awoke one morning with an idea of a ritual for healing and integration of herself, and had implemented that ritual.

The ritual began with Mary gathering containers of every size and shape. She chose them carefully to represent all the inner aspects that she had worked with. The size was significant for her. Since Mary's inner critic was large; she chose a large container for this part. The pleaser self was medium sized to reflect its significance in her current life. The adolescent self was a small size, etc. When each aspect of her was represented, Mary filled them all with water and placed them in her freezer. While they were in her freezer, she went about her daily life.

The next step became clear to Mary a few days later. She then continued the ritual by gathering all those frozen parts of herself, thanking them for their gifts to her and for all healing they had done, then emptied the ice pieces into her favorite, prized, large crystal bowl.

Mary waited for the ice to melt. When the ice was finally melted, Mary stirred the water with her favorite sterling silver spoon, then laid the spoon aside and gazed at the water in its liquid form. She gazed in love, held that bowl in love, and then and only then, did Mary drink that water. She drank of herself. She drank of her healing. She embodied herself in her very cells. Mary had become the crystal bowl.

She opened her canvas bag and taking it out said, "This very bowl." It was beautiful and shone with a vibrant light as the sun touched its numerous angles and shapes. Despite its many angles, despite its many shapes and many ways of reflecting and bending the light, this was one–one beautiful bowl.

≈

There are many doorways to healing: the body, the emotion self, the spirit. The intellect is one doorway but often only one piece of the healing, as was true for Mary.

Mary's ritual spoke strongly about healing and about integration. Mary's ritual also spoke about the importance of how we hold ourselves. We can hold the aspects of ourselves in criticism or distain. We can view things from our ego self only or from our Larger Wisdom Self, that can hold us in unconditional love. Mary was acting from her Larger Wisdom Self when she held her crystal bowl in reverence, gazed lovingly at its contents of her wholeness, and then drank that holy water and *became* the sacred container of her selves.

This Larger Wisdom is inside all of us. Sometimes we just need help to remember it, to remember who we really are, our authenticity. One thing that seems to be helpful for most of us is a daily centering practice. A daily practice is a time where we dedicate ourselves to listening for and being with that Big Picture part of us. What we do during that time, and there are many options, seems less important than that we choose to be with our Higher Self in a way that appeals and resonates with us. That is why for many people, a practice can change over time, many times, as your relationship with the Higher Self changes, too.

Options for a daily practice include centering prayer, meditation, chanting, body prayer, dance or movement. It might also be inspirational reading, a Reiki practice, a walk outdoors, using prayer beads, reading scripture, listening to inspirational music or, being in silence and listening. For Mary, journaling with her Larger Wisdom Self was the way she remembered who she was. These are just some ideas and certainly not all the choices available to us. *Everyday Spiritual Practice: Simple Pathways for Enriching Your Life* by Scott W. Alexander, is a wonderful source of practice options.

I like the image of holding myself like a full-to-the-brim, fine crystal bowl. I like the image of you holding yourself that way, too. And I like the image of one Universal Crystal Bowl that holds us all.

Reflection Questions and Journal Prompts

- *Do you have a daily centering practice where you can dedicate time to be with your Higher Self? If you do have such a practice, what is it like for you? Is it always the same or do you sometimes shift and change it?*

- *If you have a daily practice, how do you notice the impact of this in your daily life? What do you notice if you should skip or miss your daily practice?*

- *If you don't have a daily practice, can you imagine beginning one for yourself? Do you notice any resistance to this? If so, please don't judge—just notice it and maybe explore it.*

- *If you have interest in developing a daily practice, where and what do you imagine would work for you? What would you like to try first?*

- *If you were to identity some aspects of your inner self that make up the whole of you, an inner critic for example, what aspects would you name?*

- *If you name these inner aspects of yourself, would you envision them, as Mary did, different shapes and sizes? What would your containers look like?*

- *Can you imagine a ritual of integration of your inner aspects, like Mary's crystal bowl ritual, that would support you? Would you be open to that ritual? Why or why not?*

Suggested Activities or Experiences

- *You might engage in a ritual of integration of your inner aspects. Maybe you like the crystal bowl idea, or maybe there is something different that is just right for you.*

- *Maybe there is a dance of integration waiting for you.*

- *Maybe there is a time of sculpting this integration.*

- *Maybe there is an art expression piece calling you.*

- *Spend some time imagining yourself as a sacred container like the crystal bowl that holds all of you without judgment. What would your container look like, feel like, sound like?*

- *You might spend an entire day moving through your life as if you were that sacred container. You could practice knowing that you are, indeed, that sacred container.*

Meditation on Integration

Begin by finding a comfortable place to sit or lie down where you won't be disturbed. Close your eyes if that is comfortable for you. Allow your awareness to come to your breath. For now, just notice the breath. In and out, in and out. Let the breath breathe you. Be breathed by the breath. Take all the time you need right now to just be with the breath.

When you are ready, you welcome your body into this day, into this experience. Begin by bringing loving awareness to the body. Just notice the body and how it is at this moment of this day. There is no need to change anything and there is no judgment, only loving awareness of the body. Notice any places of tension, discomfort or holding. Notice any places of ease, flow and comfort. Welcome the body into this experience, this day, and breathe a breath of acceptance to the body. Only after extending awareness, welcome and acceptance to the body, do you notice if there is any tension, holding or energy in the body, that is no longer needed, that is ready to be released. If so, then you just let it go, perhaps sailing it out on the exhaled breath. If this created any new spaciousness in the body you can use your breath to expand out the health and wholeness that lives at your core into this newly opened space. You may also wish to partner that with breathing in the wholeness energy available in the larger universe outside of you. Breathing in, and expanding out health and wholeness for the body.

You can extend this same welcome to the emotion self. Begin by noticing with loving awareness whatever emotions are present with you this moment of this day. No judgment, no right or wrong, no need to change anything. For now, just notice the emotion self. Welcome the emotion self into this day. When you are ready, breathe a breath of acceptance to the emotion self, no matter what is found there. And only after this welcoming and this extending of acceptance, do you notice if there is any emotion energy that is no longer needed and is ready to be released. If there is, you just let it go. No force, no effort, just release. Perhaps you send it out with the support of the exhaled breath. Release it in whatever is your way. And if this has created any new spaciousness in your emotion self, expand out the emotional health and wholeness that lives at your core into this newly opened

space. You may also wish to partner this with breathing in the larger emotion health and wholeness energy available from the larger universe outside of you. Breathe in and expand out to fill the emotion self with health and wholeness.

You can give this same gift now to your thinking mind. Take time to pause and notice with loving awareness the thoughts and beliefs moving through your mind, along with any mental chatter present at this moment of this day. Pause to notice the thoughts without the need to engage them and perhaps remember that the thoughts are not necessarily your deeper truths. After a few moments of noticing, you welcome your thinking mind into this day and this experience. Breathe a breath of acceptance to your mind. And only after noticing, welcoming and extending acceptance, do you notice if there are any old beliefs that are no longer true for you or any mental chatter, or thoughts that are no longer needed. If there are, and they are ready to be released, just let them go. Perhaps you can do this with the support of your exhaled breath or whatever is your way. And if this creates any new spaciousness in your mind, you expand out the peace and wholeness that lives at your core to fill this space. Again, you may wish to partner this with the peace and harmony that also lives in the world outside of you. Breathing in and expanding out peace and harmony for the mind.

Now you have created an environment where your wisest Self can emerge. And so you pause and breathe and be as this Self that is your true nature. You take all the time you need to deepen your connection as this wise and expansive Self.

You may now choose to stay in this place, in this way, with your expansive Self. You might choose instead to go on a journey of integration.

If you are consciously choosing the journey of integration, you find yourself out in nature walking along a path. You notice how the path engages all of your senses.

As you continue walking you notice how excited you are to be traveling to a place that is named, "The Place of Integration." Along the way you encounter various aspects of your inner self. Perhaps you come upon your inner critic; perhaps you come upon your inner achiever, your worrier or others. As you encounter these various personality aspects you welcome them to the journey of exploration and you all continue on together.

At the perfect time you notice the path opens up into the area that you know is the place you have been waiting for, The Place of Integration. You feel a sense of safety here. You are immediately *aware that in this place are all the items needed for your own perfect ritual, or ceremony, of integration. As all the aspects of you step forward you also notice the presence of any other support needed to witness you in this ritual. And so your ritual or ceremony of integration unfolds in a way that brings together all the aspects of your wholeness.*

As each aspect of your wholeness is integrated into the whole you notice that each aspect is now present in a balanced form. In this way you are amazed at how these aspects now can assist you in your life journey. Instead of bullying you, the critic can now offer healthy critique. Your worrier no longer keeps you filled with anxiety but rather offers healthy caution. Each aspect offers itself to this experience and transforms into a balanced wholeness that is you in your wisest form. If an aspect needs something before its integration, it is provided. At the right pace and time, there is a perfect closure or culmination of your ceremony in which you behold yourself in all your luminous wholeness. You may even have a glimpse of how being in the world in this way will be different for you.

When the time is right, you give gratitude for your experience. You are given a symbol, word or visual image that you take with you to remember your wholeness and the sense of yourself in an integrated state. When you are ready, as your integrated self, you journey in wholeness back to the place in nature where you first entered the path. At this place you turn and look back, knowing that you can return to The Place of Integration anytime you need to remember who you are. Perhaps you bow in honor of your experience and this place.

When it is time, you begin to shift your awareness to where you first began this meditation. You notice the surface upon which you began this meditation. You take several comfortably deep breaths and when you are ready you open your eyes, knowing that this experience has served you in powerful ways.

You may wish to journal about your integration experience or share with a trusted companion.

POLISHED BY LIFE

The summer I was diagnosed with breast cancer, a friend and her daughter came over to my house to offer their support and prayers. They had been part of my journey for some time—the daughter had even asked for prayers on my behalf on Facebook—but this was the first time we had come together since my diagnosis. They came carrying a tiny box wrapped in bright paper and tied with a vibrant ribbon. After we chatted awhile, they were eager for me to open that little gift. Inside, resting in delicate tissue paper was a pair of bright, shiny earrings made of white stone. The earrings came from California, where they had been visiting when they heard of my diagnosis. The earrings were so lovely and they reflected the light in a way that seemed almost magical. As I lifted them out of the box, I noticed a piece of paper that described these moonstones. It said something like this:

Moonstones in their uncut state are rather unimpressive and have not yet revealed the mysterious shimmer for which they are known. Light rays are scattered and refracted inside the stone but this quality is only revealed upon polishing. Moonstones are said to bring protection to those of a sensitive nature, as well as good fortune and inner strength. Polishing can be intentional, as when a jeweler might tend them, or it can happen naturally, as when the stones are tossed and turned and thrown, again and yet again, by the surf until they land upon the shore.

I love this metaphor of tossing and turning, of battering by a strong force, then ultimately revealing a mysterious glow and shimmer in something then considered precious. I wore these earrings, intentionally inviting the gift of inner strength and protection, while I felt the tossing and turning of surgery, radiation, and testing. And I opened to the polishing of my body-spirit and welcomed whatever shimmer, mysterious or not, might find me.

The week leading up to my diagnostic mammograms now is a time where I find I am slightly holding my breath and noticing a bit of tension since my journey with my former breast cancer. While most of me is aware that my cancer is unlikely to reoccur, there remains a small part of me that worries. And so, with compassion and tender care, I try to consciously support that part. Each year now, the week before my mammogram, I open my jewelry box, take out the precious moonstone earrings, and remind myself of my own preciousness. I open to strength, to protection. I claim the shimmer from the "polishing" of the past years, and I wear the earrings each day that week.

≈

Mysteriously, moonstones were part of two powerful sessions with clients that very week one year. For one, I met with a woman for the first time for a spiritual companion session. Since it was our initial session, it was a time of deciding if we were a good partnership to support her spiritual journey. She had received my name from a friend she respected, and when she Googled me, the prayer request of my friend's daughter popped up. From that Facebook post, she learned that I'd had breast cancer and this helped her feel safe to share her own recent serious health challenge and her journey with it.

Our session was a good one, and as we wrapped up our time together, she asked about my earrings. I shared their story, and she got tears in her eyes and mentioned she had received a moonstone pendant during her illness and that it had brought her comfort, though she did not know the meaning behind the stones. Together, we appreciated the ways we are gifted with just what we need even if we don't understand a gift's significance at the time we receive it.

Another session that same week brought me together with a wise, young woman who was consciously trying to again find her inner strength and wisdom after a time of feeling lost. In previous sessions, we had pondered ways she might remember her own wisdom and the larger wisdom all around her on a daily basis. She took seriously an invitation to try out various ideas and shared her exploration of those possibilities. One in particular had been quite powerful for her. She had always been rock collector, she said, and she had placed several stones on top of picture frames in her apartment. During the past week, she had taken down the stones from the frames, washed, and dusted them. Of all the stones, she was particularly drawn to a moonstone. She found that carrying this in her pocket over the past week was a good reminder of that larger, inner wisdom. When she told me this, I just smiled. I had my moonstone earrings on, and told her their story. Together, we marveled in the ways we beings are connected beyond intellect, beyond cognitive knowing, beyond rational thought, beyond even the best of our human planning. We celebrated synchronicity, the way seemingly unrelated events come together offering deep meaning.

Mysterious shimmer, magical glow . . . we are all being polished by the many ways life tumbles us.

Reflection Questions and Journal Prompts

- *What speaks to you from this story?*

- *What places in your life have you felt a tossing and turning, and maybe even a rough battering, upon the shore of life?*

- *Can you speak to the ways that this battering may have polished you, given you a mysterious glow?*

- *What supported you in moving from the "battering" to "polishing"?*

- *What talismans or objects do you carry, or might you carry, to remind you of your wisdom, strength and protection?*

- *Can you claim some places of synchronicity or mysterious coincidences that remind you of the Larger Wisdom at work and play in your life?*

Suggested Activities or Experiences

- *Perhaps you are able to go to the ocean and watch the surf's strong force bringing in and washing out. Imagine a stone being polished by this action of the tide. Imagine that similar force polishing you in your own life through a challenge place.*

- *Perhaps you wish to find a polished stone to carry as a way of reminding you of your own polishing from life's challenges.*

- *Write a poem; make a drawing or do a dance or movement about polishing.*

- *Take one day where you practice walking and being in the world as a polished being that shines with a mysterious glow. Notice what that experience is like for you. You may wish to journal about your experience of this day.*

Meditation on Being Polished

Begin by finding a comfortable place to sit or lie down where you won't be disturbed. Close your eyes if that is comfortable for you. Allow your awareness to come to your breath. For now, just notice the breath. In and out, in and out. Let the breath breathe you. Be breathed by the breath. Take all the time you need right now to just be with the breath.

And when you are ready, you welcome your body into this day, into this experience. Begin by bringing loving awareness to the body. Just notice how the body is at this moment of the day. There is no need to change anything and there is no judgment, only loving awareness of the body. Notice any places of tension, discomfort or holding. Notice any places of ease, flow and comfort in the body. Welcome the body into this experience, this day and breathe a breath of acceptance to the body. Only after extending awareness, welcome and acceptance to the body do you notice if there is any tension, holding or energy in the body, that is no longer needed, that is ready to be released. If so, then you just let it go, perhaps sailing it out on the exhaled breath. And if this created any new spaciousness in the body, you can use your breath to expand out the health and wholeness that lives at your core into this newly opened space. You may also wish to partner that with breathing in the wholeness energy available in the larger universe outside of you. Breathing in, and expanding out health and wholeness for the body.

You can extend this same welcome to the emotion self. Begin by noticing with loving awareness whatever emotions are present with you this moment of this day. No judgment, no right or wrong, no need to change anything. For now just notice the emotion self. Welcome the emotion self into this day. When you are ready, breathe a breath of acceptance to the emotion self no matter what is found there. And only after this welcoming and this extending of acceptance do you notice if there is any emotion energy that is no longer needed that is ready to be released. And if there is, you just let it go. Don't force. Don't effort. Just release. Perhaps you send it out with the support of the exhaled breath. Release it in whatever is your way. And if this has created any new spaciousness in your emotion self you expand out the emotional health and wholeness that lives at your core into this newly opened

space. You may also wish to partner this with breathing in the larger emotion health and wholeness energy available from the larger universe outside of you. Breathe in and expand out to fill the emotion self with health and wholeness.

You can give this same gift now to your thinking mind. Take time to pause and notice with loving awareness the thoughts and beliefs moving through the mind along with noticing any mental chatter present at this moment of this day. Pause to notice the thoughts without the need to engage them and perhaps remember that the thoughts are not necessarily your deeper truths. After a few moments of noticing you welcome your thinking mind into this day and this experience. Breathe a breath of acceptance to your mind. And only after noticing, welcoming and extending acceptance do you notice if there are any old beliefs that are no longer true for you or any mental chatter or thoughts that are no longer needed. If there are, and they are ready to be released, you just let them go. Perhaps with the support of your exhaled breath or whatever is your way. And if this creates any new spaciousness in your mind, you expand out the peace and wholeness that lives at your core to fill this space. Again, you may wish to partner this with the peace and harmony that also lives in the world outside of you. Breathing in and expanding out peace and harmony for the mind.

Now you have created an environment where your wisest Self can emerge. And so you pause and breathe and be as this Self that is your true nature. You take all the time you need deepening your connection as this wise and expansive Self.

You can now choose to remain here with your wise Self or you may choose to go on a journey of being polished.

If you are choosing to go on the journey of being polished, in your mind's eye now, you imagine yourself on a beach where there is a tide moving in and out, in and out. You attune all your senses to this place. You notice the sounds of this surf. You are aware of the ocean breezes on your skin. You notice the taste of salt on your lips. And you take in all the images before you.

You connect now with the part of yourself that yearns to reveal its mysterious shimmer. You access the part of you that wishes to bring out healthy protection, good fortune and inner strength. In a way that is completely safe for you, with all the support that you need at your disposal, you prepare to enter the surf with the intention of being polished.

When you are ready, you enter the water. You go out as far as feels just right for you. You allow the water to hold you up. You give yourself, in a safe way, to the water and to the surf. You find yourself being carried in and out with the tide in a way that is just right for you. As the waves toss you, you surrender to this back and forth motion. Over time, you begin to notice that you are feeling your inner strength in a new and powerful way. You notice that you feel even more protection around you and inside of you. Perhaps you also notice a growing sense of inner optimism. And you notice that you are glowing. There is a luminous, shimmering light that is radiating from your core out into the water and air.

You claim yourself as moonstone. You claim yourself as polished by life. You claim yourself as precious. You claim your inner strength and the quality of protection. You open to the good fortune available to you. You are radiant, shimmering light. And you are grateful.

When you are ready you exit the water and move up onto the shore. Here you pause, taking time to integrate your experience.

Honoring your own pace and timing you give gratitude to all that has supported you including the source of the polishing and your willingness to be polished. As you are ready you say goodbye to the water and the surf. You return now to the place where you first began your meditation.

You feel your body supported by the surface of where you began this meditation. You begin bringing your awareness back to the time a place where you began. You take some comfortable deep breaths and open your eyes when you are ready.

You take all the time you need to process your meditation. You may wish to journal or share your experience of being polished with a friend.

BEING THE TEACHING

It was June. It was hot and humid. I could feel the oppressive air draped over me like a heavy, wet wool cape. We were between sessions at a holistic conference on a University of Wisconsin campus when the sound of a tornado siren pierced the air. Everyone scattered to the nearest building and that's how I found myself in the basement hallway of the cafeteria.

There were hundreds of us. We were packed like sardines. We were hot. We were sweaty. You could feel the tension, anxiety and fear. There was a lot of talking, loudly, and none of it seemed very positive. As a person sensitive to others' feelings and energy, I began to feel as if a dismal, pressing weight had been placed over me. It was all I could do just to keep breathing.

And then I noticed him. Right across from me was Chunyi Lin, the founder of Spring Forest Qigong, a Chinese healing practice. My partner had planned to take a class from him, and so I recognized him as one of the main presenters from the brochure.

Lin sat down. Just simply sat down and closed his eyes in the mere inches allowed for each of us. Instantly, I felt calm radiate out from him. I felt calmer and watched with curiosity as other's voices began to quiet. Those who were still talking were now using their indoor voices. It was as if a stone of serenity had been dropped in the pond of that hallway and ripple after ripple of calm radiated out. Soon the crowded hallway was one of the most tranquil places I have ever been. I was amazed.

What was most astounding to me was that not one word about calming down and finding our center was spoken, and yet this was the largest teaching I had ever witnessed about being calm and finding our center. I realized that Chunyi Lin was indeed a master of qigong, but more than that, he was a master of teaching by *being the teaching*.

≈

Barney, our 18-year-old cat, has long black-and-white fur that she sheds wherever she wants to. She was named after the purple dinosaur by her owners during the first three years of her life and we didn't have the heart to change it even though she's not purple, she's not male and she's not a dinosaur. She came to us when domestic violence precipitated a move by a mother and child to a shelter that didn't allow pets. When they couldn't take her back we were given a huge gift of her presence in our home. That was fifteen years ago and she never ceases to amaze me. Barney can be snoozing by the sliding screen door for hours. But when a small ground squirrel comes to visit she jumps up, sounds a serious hiss and protects her territory as if she had been on security watch all along. Barney is a great example of how to be calm and relaxed and yet ready to be alert at a moment's notice. Barney teaches me this by *being the teaching.*

≈

I take the back way to my office in the morning. I pull off busy streets into a residential area and, rain or shine, there he is. He has a small stature, tiny little wire-rimmed glasses, and looks to be about 4 or 5 years old. His backpack is always with him. Sometimes he wears it, and it appears heavy enough to tip him over. Other days the backpack rests on the ground beside him. His head is often pointed down and sometimes he is kneeling. He is frequently engaged with the flowers that grow beside the large rock on the corner. He sometimes seems to speak to the insects he lifts from the blossoms. He touches the rock and I imagine he is sensing its temperature. One day, he sits on top of the rock, another day he leans against it while he waits. He takes it all in, everything. He is intent, content, right where he is. I don't know where he is going, and it doesn't matter. I don't know his name or if he lives in the house on that corner. I don't know who is watching over him, if anyone. He is not focused on these things and neither am I. What I do know is that he is my teacher. He teaches me to savor what is before me as I enter my workday. He is my reminder to go slow, to soak up this day, to wait with wonder and presence. He teaches me to wait with grace and consciousness. He teaches me to come home to the deep river of peace within me and within this day. He teaches me by *being the teaching.*

I've had many teachers in my life, who have used many teaching methods. And I have learned many things, but it has only been in the past decade that I have learned what it means to teach by *being the teaching*. It's a remarkable thing, really. It has made me realize that I want to be that kind of teacher, and I now ponder what I can teach by being the teaching. I hope to be the teaching of how to hold the paradoxes, the both/ands of life. I hope to be the teaching of holding fear *and* love, yes *and* no, this *and* that simultaneously. I hope I am a teacher of living what we're called to do by doing that very thing, even when it is scary and intimidating. I hope I am a teacher of how to hold others in sacred space by offering that. And I hope that, ultimately, I am a teacher of love by being the presence of love to all living things and beings. This is my prayer.

Reflection Questions and Journal Prompts

- *What, if anything, speaks to you from these stories?*

- *Who have you witnessed in your life that is the teaching?*

- *What is your prayer about how to "be the teaching"? What is your prayer about what it is that you wish to "be the teaching" of?*

- *What supports do you desire in your life so that you may live out this prayer?*

Suggested Activities or Experiences

- *You might write your prayer for "being the teaching." You might express this prayer through art or movement.*

- *You might spend a significant amount of time being on the lookout for those who are "being the teaching." If you are around these people, just notice how it is to be in their presence.*

- *You might intentionally spend your days living your own "being the teaching" prayer. Notice how it is to be in your own presence.*

Meditation on Being the Teaching

Begin by finding a comfortable place to sit or lie down where you won't be disturbed. Close your eyes if that is comfortable for you. Allow your awareness to come to your breath. For now, just notice the breath. In and out, in and out. Let the breath breathe you. Be breathed by the breath. Take all the time you need right now to just be with the breath.

And when you are ready, you welcome your body into this day, into this experience. Begin by bringing loving awareness to the body. Just notice how the body is at this moment of the day. There is no need to change anything and there is no judgment, only loving awareness of the body. Notice any places of tension, discomfort or holding. Notice any places of ease, flow and comfort in the body. Welcome the body into this experience, this day and breathe a breath of acceptance to the body. Only after extending awareness, welcome and acceptance to the body do you notice if there is any tension, holding or energy in the body, that is no longer needed, that is ready to be released. If so, then you just let it go, perhaps sailing it out on the exhaled breath. And if this created any new spaciousness in the body, you can use your breath to expand out the health and wholeness that lives at your core into this newly opened space. You may also wish to partner that with breathing in the wholeness energy available in the larger universe outside of you. Breathing in, and expanding out health and wholeness for the body.

You can extend this same welcome to the emotion self. Begin by noticing with loving awareness whatever emotions are present with you this moment of this day. No judgment, no right or wrong, no need to change anything. For now just notice the emotion self. Welcome the emotion self into this day. When you are ready, breathe a breath of acceptance to the emotion self no matter what is found there. And only after this welcoming and this extending of acceptance do you notice if there is any emotion energy that is no longer needed that is ready to be released. And if there is, you just let it go. Don't force. Don't effort. Just release. Perhaps you send it out with the support of the exhaled breath. Release it in whatever is your way. And if this has created any new spaciousness in your emotion self you expand out the emotional health and wholeness that lives at your core into this newly opened

space. You may also wish to partner this with breathing in the larger emotion health and wholeness energy available from the larger universe outside of you. Breathe in and expand out to fill the emotion self with health and wholeness.

You can give this same gift now to your thinking mind. Take time to pause and notice with loving awareness the thoughts and beliefs moving through the mind along with noticing any mental chatter present at this moment of this day. Pause to notice the thoughts without the need to engage them and perhaps remember that the thoughts are not necessarily your deeper truths. After a few moments of noticing you welcome your thinking mind into this day and this experience. Breathe a breath of acceptance to your mind. And only after noticing, welcoming and extending acceptance do you notice if there are any old beliefs that are no longer true for you or any mental chatter or thoughts that are no longer needed. If there are, and they are ready to be released, you just let them go. Perhaps with the support of your exhaled breath or whatever is your way. And if this creates any new spaciousness in your mind, you expand out the peace and wholeness that lives at your core to fill this space. Again, you may wish to partner this with the peace and harmony that also lives in the world outside of you. Breathing in and expanding out peace and harmony for the mind.

Now you have created an environment where your wisest Self can emerge. And so you pause and breathe and be as this Self that is your true nature. You take all the time you need deepening your connection as this wise and expansive Self.

As, always, you can choose to remain here relaxing with your wise Self. You can also choose to go on a journey of being the teaching.

If you choose the journey of being the teaching, in your mind's eye you find yourself at a place in nature that feels safe for you. You are aware that all your senses pleasantly enjoy this place. In this place you pause and contemplate the ways in which you are called to be the teaching. Whether or not you are consciously aware of these ways, you make a commitment to journey to the place where you can welcome your presence as being the teaching.

And so you begin that journey, following whatever path or route leads you to this special being the teaching place. Here you find all the support and items you need for a special being the teaching ceremony. In a way just right for you a ceremony unfolds. Perhaps there are special words or music. Perhaps there are special witnesses present. Perhaps you are led through a sacred and safe ritual of a being the teaching initiation. Whatever unfolds you find deep meaning and an inner shift inside that is about claiming your own unique way of being the teaching to which you are called.

You are aware of an inner shift that you recognize as a commitment to being the presence of this teaching in the world. You may even be given a special symbol, object or word that will help you remember this commitment when you forget. You may even find that you are given a glimpse of yourself being this teaching in the world and its impact upon others and the world. You find yourself present for this entire experience, all the way through to completion.

At the closure of your ceremony there is time to give gratitude and all the time you need to really anchor this experience deep within you.

When you are ready you leave this special place knowing that you are changed by the experience. You take the same path and return to where you first began your journey of being the teaching. At this place you may give gratitude once again.

When the time is right you begin to bring your awareness back to the place where you first began this meditation. You feel the support of your body. You take several comfortably deep breaths and open your eyes when you are ready. You invite this meditation experience to be lived in the ordinary world.

You may wish to journal about your experience or share with a trusted friend or companion.

THE HUMMINGBIRD'S GIFT

We tried for years to attract hummingbirds to our yard. We purchased special feeders, tried sugar-water recipes and dyed the water red. We bought special packaged food for hummingbirds. We tried different kinds of hummingbird feeders and planted all the flowers the experts said would attract them. For years we watched and waited. And yet there were no hummingbirds to be found.

Then came the spring and summer when my father was dying and I was in deep grief. I would sit on our deck and take time to be present in my grief. One fine, sunny day early in my father's journey, I was on the deck and crying heavily. All of a sudden, out of nowhere, guess who paid me a visit? The hummingbirds I had longed for and worked so hard to attract had finally come to me during this very difficult time.

In Ted Andrew's book, *Animal Speak*, it is said that hummingbirds bring a reminder to find our nectar, our sweetness in life, even in the most difficult of circumstances. And so the hummingbird became a reminder from Divine Presence and my dad that no matter what happened, it would be okay. It was a reminder that I could still find joy and happiness amidst this intense grief.

I saw that hummingbird many times that spring and summer, and not just when I was on the deck. Sometimes I would be in the house talking to Dad on the phone and I would see my friend, the hummingbird, out the front window. Each time a wave of tranquility would wash over me.

Eight months after my dad died, my niece graduated from high school. Before leaving to attend her celebration, I had a talk with Dad's spirit.

"Dad," I said, "I know you'll be there for your favorite granddaughter in spirit. But if you could send a sign that would be really cool. Maybe a hummingbird."

"A hummingbird," I thought. "Well, maybe that's asking for too much."

So I corrected myself. "I know that asking for that hummingbird might be too much, Dad, so just send any message at all and I'll be grateful."

We arrived at my mom's house for the party and went out on her deck for some iced tea. No sooner were we seated than a hummingbird flew right up on the deck and began to feed at some nearby flowers. My mom swore she'd never had hummingbirds in her yard before.

The next day, we were at my sister's house to celebrate my niece. Her party was outside on their deck, and I was standing at the railing when another visit from the hummingbird gifted us. My sister swore they hadn't seen hummingbirds in their yard before that day.

"Thanks, Dad, and thank you, hummingbird." I said in my heart.

Most of all, thanks to you, Everywhere Presence, for your many gifts and for reminding me that you always send what we need—even when we think it's too much.

Reflection Questions and Journal Prompts

- *What, if anything, touches you about this story?*

- *Have you had experiences or heard stories of similar happenings? If so, did you share them with others? Why or why not?*

- *What do you think of mystical experiences that may not be able to be logically understood?*

Suggested Activities or Experiences

- *You might consider, if you haven't already, asking friends and family about their own mystical experiences.*

- *You might consider, if you haven't already, sharing your own mystical experiences with family or friends.*

- *You might consciously ask for more mystical experiences to make themselves known to you.*

- *You might dedicate one full day to being open to the mysticism all around you, letting go of any expectations about what that might look like.*

- *You might explore mysticism and mystics in literature and the arts.*

Meditation on Receiving What We Need

Begin by finding a comfortable place to sit or lie down where you won't be disturbed. Close your eyes if that is comfortable for you. Allow your awareness to come to your breath. For now, just notice the breath. In and out, in and out. Let the breath breathe you. Be breathed by the breath. Take all the time you need right now to just be with the breath.

And when you are ready, you welcome your body into this day, into this experience. Begin by bringing loving awareness to the body. Just notice how the body is at this moment of the day. There is no need to change anything and there is no judgment, only loving awareness of the body. Notice any places of tension, discomfort or holding. Notice any places of ease, flow and comfort in the body. Welcome the body into this experience, this day and breathe a breath of acceptance to the body. Only after extending awareness, welcome and acceptance to the body do you notice if there is any tension, holding or energy in the body, that is no longer needed, that is ready to be released. If so, then you just let it go, perhaps sailing it out on the exhaled breath. And if this created any new spaciousness in the body, you can use your breath to expand out the health and wholeness that lives at your core into this newly opened space. You may also wish to partner that with breathing in the wholeness energy available in the larger universe outside of you. Breathing in, and expanding out health and wholeness for the body.

You can extend this same welcome to the emotion self. Begin by noticing with loving awareness whatever emotions are present with you this moment of this day. No judgment, no right or wrong, no need to change anything. For now just notice the emotion self. Welcome the emotion self into this day. When you are ready, breathe a breath of acceptance to the emotion self no matter what is found there. And only after this welcoming and this extending of acceptance do you notice if there is any emotion energy that is no longer needed that is ready to be released. And if there is, you just let it go. Don't force. Don't effort. Just release. Perhaps you send it out with the support of the exhaled breath. Release it in whatever is your way. And if this has created any new spaciousness in your emotion self you expand out the emotional health and wholeness that lives at your core into this newly opened

space. You may also wish to partner this with breathing in the larger emotion health and wholeness energy available from the larger universe outside of you. Breathe in and expand out to fill the emotion self with health and wholeness.

You can give this same gift now to your thinking mind. Take time to pause and notice with loving awareness the thoughts and beliefs moving through the mind along with noticing any mental chatter present at this moment of this day. Pause to notice the thoughts without the need to engage them and perhaps remember that the thoughts are not necessarily your deeper truths. After a few moments of noticing you welcome your thinking mind into this day and this experience. Breathe a breath of acceptance to your mind. And only after noticing, welcoming and extending acceptance do you notice if there are any old beliefs that are no longer true for you or any mental chatter or thoughts that are no longer needed. If there are, and they are ready to be released, you just let them go. Perhaps with the support of your exhaled breath or whatever is your way. And if this creates any new spaciousness in your mind, you expand out the peace and wholeness that lives at your core to fill this space. Again, you may wish to partner this with the peace and harmony that also lives in the world outside of you. Breathing in and expanding out peace and harmony for the mind.

Now you have created an environment where your wisest Self can emerge. And so you pause and breathe and be as this Self that is your true nature. You take all the time you need deepening your connection as this wise and expansive Self.

You can now choose to remain relaxing with your wise Self or you may choose to take a journey of receiving all that you need.

If you are choosing to take the journey, you find yourself in a place that is safe for you. Perhaps you are in nature. Perhaps you are in a room or building that is special to you. Wherever you find yourself, you notice that this place is pleasant to all of your senses. In this place you pause to reflect on some area of your life to which you wish to bring more peace, acceptance or possibility. As this issue becomes clear, you allow yourself to relax. In the relaxed state you allow your eyes to close if that is comfortable for you. You release all expectations. You take all the time you need to breathe consciously in and out of your heart center, or experience some other way your heart, as it softens, opens and becomes receptive.

When you are ready you open your eyes and bring your full attention to the image of your situation that is now right there before you. Only this time, there is something different about your situation.

There has been some kind of surprise unfolding. Perhaps there is someone there with you offering whatever is needed. Perhaps something is added that offers a new perspective, a way to see with new eyes. Perhaps you find something inside of you has shifted mysteriously. Whatever unexpected possibilities arise in whatever way, you find that all that you require is somehow available to you and for you. You are able now to experience more peace, more acceptance, more possibility, more of whatever you require to be with whatever you are called to in your situation.

You take all the time you need to integrate your new experience in every fiber of your being. You trust that whatever has unfolded is just right for this time, place, and issue in your life. You give gratitude for your experience, whatever it is.

When the time to leave approaches you may find that there is a symbol, object, word or image that you take with you to remember this experience.

You gather all that you are taking with you and anchor it deep inside in your own way. Honoring your own pace and time, when you are ready, you begin to leave this special place and return to the place where you first began this meditation. You bring your awareness back to your breath and the environment where you began this meditation time. When you are ready you open your eyes. You take all the time you need to integrate your experience before entering the next part of your day.

You may wish to journal about your experience or share it with a trusted friend or companion.

PART TWO:

Turning Around the Heart of Connection

We open to connection. When we connect beyond our differences, with the wisdom of the body, our intuition, our explorations, our softness, our life's dangers and opportunities, in sacred places and with those who have come before us, we can open to connection with our self, others and the larger universe in surprising ways.

ANYONE FOR ICE CREAM?

A friend blessed me with this true story years ago. This is how I remember it. May it care for you the way it has cared for me.

Allan and I sat on a sun-filled patio at the edge of the Gulf of Mexico. As we shared family joys and sorrows, he began to tell of his relationship with his sister, Ann. They were different in every imaginable way: she was conservative, he was liberal. She followed mainstream religion. He favored Native American spirituality. He described her as rigid and narrow in her beliefs. He claimed to be pretty wide in his ways of tolerance. She expressed disdain for higher education. He had his Master's Degree in three fields. Discord rang on every subject, every level. They had grown up in conflict and carried that way of relating right on into their adulthood. But on one summer day, they were joined through the magic of ice cream.

Allan and Ann both knew their grandmother was close to death. Her physical health was deteriorating almost as rapidly as her memory. So, on that one hot summer day, Allan and his sister put aside their differences and went together to visit their grandmother at the nursing home.

They weren't allowed to take Grandma outside, so the three of them sat in her small, stuffy room, cramped with too much furniture. She didn't recognize them and stared off into a distant place. She seemed lost in her own little world. Allan and his sister talked about the special memories they had with Grandma. They spoke of birthday parties, walks in the park, books that were read, and so on. They giggled about the times Grandma would take them for ice cream—big, drippy, double-decker cones. Time after time, she would patiently wipe the drops of stickiness from their chins.

As they shared this memory, Allan and Ann noticed that Grandma, with clear and focused eyes, began to look at them and smile. It was obvious the story had triggered some pleasant memory for her, too. In that instant, Allan and his sister saw beyond their disagreements and both knew at once what they would do. Without speaking a word, they got Grandma a sweater and lap cover; one checked the hallway for security and the other stood ready at the helm of the wheelchair. Then they dashed out the back door. All three were laughing and giggling breathlessly as the wind blew their hair. Two blocks later, Grandma had her ice cream and neither Allan nor his sister minded wiping the weathered face and hands just as lovingly as she had done for them years before. She was returned to her room with a lingering smile and no ill effects from the outing.

≈

Which stories we tell makes a difference. Telling stories of grief, for example, can help us honor our grief and perhaps move the healing process along. Telling stories of difficulty, discord, challenge and tragedy can help us integrate and learn from those experiences, too. The way we tell the stories also makes a difference. Which stories we share and how we share them can stretch us beyond old beliefs, old ways of relating from our small or ego self. Stories can also bring us back home to our largest, expansive, and Higher Consciousness Self.

Through the magic of story and ice cream Grandma returned for a time to the present moment, Allan and Ann found a way of bridging the long and bitter gulf between them, and one last happy memory of Grandma was forever anchored in their hearts and minds. Anyone for ice cream?

Reflection Questions and Journal Prompts

- *What touches you about this story?*

- *Are there people in your life with whom you have felt estranged because of differences? How would you describe those differences? Are there stories with these people that you find yourself telling and retelling? What do you notice about your inner process with the retelling?*

- *Where in your life have you found reconciliation despite differences? How did you get there?*

- *Allan and his sister re-connected around the memories with grandma that elicited a sense of deep love. What guiding principles in your life can be unifying? Has story played a part in this for you? Which stories?*

- *What do you think about the rule breaking in this story? How do you discern when, and what, rules can be broken?*

- *Do you ever ponder your own aging? Who would be there for you? What memories or stories might be a bridge of connection between you?*

- *Is there anyone in your life right now with whom you feel an urge to reconnect? What could be your next step in that direction if it is wise for you?*

Story Telling Awareness Meditation

Gather your journal and writing implement and just have it near you in case you wish to write after this exploration.

Sit or lie down in a comfortable place where you will be undisturbed. Allow yourself to relax in body, emotion and spirit. Allow full and easy breaths to bring you to that calm and wise center within you. Take all the time you desire to breathe, be and center.

In this calm center, allow a memory or story to arise of a difficult relationship experience. Imagine telling this story to another person as perhaps you have already done. As you imagine this, notice with loving awareness how this is for your body. Notice what emotion is evoked and what thoughts or beliefs accompany the telling. Notice whether the telling of the story in this way elicits a sense of separation or resentment with the person involved in the story, or if it elicits a sense of neutrality or increased closeness. There is no right outcome here, only noticing. Allow yourself to notice if it seems as though this telling is coming from the presence in your Highest Self or from the smaller or ego self. There is no judgment, only awareness.

If you find that the telling of this story elicits discomfort for your body, emotion self or mind, or if there is less than a sense of neutrality with this person, you might let yourself imagine a way that this experience could be different for these parts of you and perhaps for the relationship, if that is the highest good. Let yourself imagine telling the story in a way that helps you access your true essence or larger Self. Is there a part of the story that could be told differently? Is there a way you could change the ending? Could you imagine bringing a new element into the story? Or could you tell a different story of an experience with this person. Trust yourself to know a way in which a shift might be offered for you. Let yourself experiment and notice. Just keep bringing your awareness back to how this shift in the telling of the same story, or the telling of a different story, offers your body, emotions and mind a different experience. Notice if the shifting might even offer a different part of you to tell the story.

When you are ready, allow your senses to reconnect with the place where you first began this meditation. Breathe and acclimate back to this place.

You may journal about your experience if you wish.

KNIT TOGETHER IN PERFECT ARTISTRY

Here I share the miraculous connection of three people, three stories and three strands knit together in perfect artistry.

Joyce, a kind woman of faith, was involved in a prayer shawl ministry in her small town. She knitted shawls to comfort people and while she knitted, she would pray for the good of the wearer. Once completed, the shawls were blessed by her church's minister. Joyce became aware, through a colleague of mine, that I saw people for spiritual guidance, psychological therapy, emotional support, and, sometimes, physical comfort. She offered a prayer shawl for my office in hope that it might bring solace to my clients.

Months after donating the prayer shawl, Joyce scheduled her own appointment with me. She began our session by showing me a photo of her husband, John. He had been diagnosed with heart failure and the prognosis wasn't good. Through his cardiologist, he was involved in some experimental treatment and might also need to undergo a risky surgery for an additional health challenge. Joyce was understandably very afraid. Over time, she admitted that in some ways she felt powerless to help John. Later, Joyce also confessed in a slightly embarrassed way, that at times *she* had found herself questioning whether her prayer shawls were of any value. But after knitting one for John, she discovered the true value of the shawls' ability to provide real and solid comfort to those in fear and crisis. When she saw her own husband wrapped in the shawl and witnessed the calm on his face, she came to *believe* in the importance of the shawl ministry.

≈

A couple of weeks later, Cheryl, a woman in her sixties, came in for an appointment. She had been seeing me for psycho-spiritual support. Her faith and resilience were amazing, and had been tested many times over the decades. Since birth, physical deformities of her hands and feet had meant reliance on wheel chairs and certain courage to fend off curious stares.

On one particular visit to my office, Cheryl had returned from a hospital visit where she had undergone intrusive procedures with the hope of reducing pain in her limbs. Her hands were thickly bandaged and undeniable facial tension made it clear that pain relief was not yet a reality. As if the intense pain wasn't enough, Cheryl told me that shortly after surgery, during some post-operative evaluation, she experienced a flashback of earlier childhood trauma. During the flashbacks and the anguish that accompanied it, she was forcefully held down by the medical staff. Although they were just trying to help her, she ended up feeling even more traumatized. Cheryl was more discouraged and hopeless than I'd ever seen her. Her previous determination and courage seemed distant. She was questioning, "Why?" "How much more can I take?" "Can I really keep going on?" and "What's the point?"

Near the end of our time together, knowing her as a deeply spiritual person, I asked Cheryl if she would be willing to wear the prayer shawl given to me earlier by Joyce. Cheryl agreed. Within minutes she was visibly calmer and her breathing had slowed. Not an uncommon request, Cheryl asked if we could pray together. She asked for guidance, the courage to keep going and pain relief. After her prayer Cheryl described feeling the tangible divine love present in the prayer shawl, in the room and now inside of her. In this place of grace, Cheryl felt she could hold all of her questions without a need for immediate answers. As we brought our session to a close, we gave gratitude. It was at that moment I felt a clear sense of spiritual guidance telling me to give Cheryl the shawl. That she was to take it with her. It was to be hers for ongoing comfort and remembering that she was not alone. I offered her the shawl and it was just like Cheryl to worry, "What will happen to the others coming here who need it?" This led to a discussion about trust and knowing that the Holy provides in some way for us all. As we moved to the waiting area where she waited for her husband to pick her up, she wore her shawl.

When we arrived in the waiting area, I was surprised to see John, Joyce's husband. He was there to see his massage therapist in the same building. He looked gaunt and weak from his illness and treatments. In his warm and loving voice, John looked at Cheryl. "I have a prayer shawl like that. When I put it on I feel safe and comforted. I remember that I am not alone and that everything will be alright." Cheryl smiled and thanked him for what she heard as words of comfort and reassurance.

After Cheryl left, John asked me to sit with him for a moment. We were both deeply moved by the synchronicity of him recognizing another of his wife's prayer shawls providing light in a time of darkness. John shared that he had been questioning the meaning of his own life as he was immersed in difficult treatments. He was clearly moved by being able to offer someone else comfort. "My problem is minor compared to hers," he said. "What I have could kill me, but *she* has real problems." With tears in our eyes, we sat together marveling at all the goodness and grace surrounding us and the opportunity to remember what is really important in our lives.

Three people, three stories, three strands of God's work, *knit* together in perfect artistry with beauty, wisdom and divine timing. Prayer shawls, powerful medicine.

Reflection Questions and Journal Prompts

- *Does this story touch you? If so, in what way?*

- *This story speaks to me about moments of unexpected grace. What are your own stories of unexpected grace?*

- *Can you recall times in your own life where you have felt yourself deeply discouraged? What guided you through those times?*

- *Can you recall a time in your life where you questioned the very meaning of your life? Who or what was a comfort to you then.*

- *Where have you been a presence of comfort for others who are discouraged or questioning the meaning of their lives?*

- *Are there places in your life right now where you might welcome in even more comfort or holding of your story? Who or what might assist you.*

Prayer Shawl Meditation

Begin by finding a place to relax where you will not be disturbed. Find a comfortable place to sit or lie down. As you enter this meditation time, allow yourself to take comfortable deep breaths. Let your breath center you. Let your breath support your release of any physical tension. Let your breath support you in releasing any emotional tension. And let your breath support you in releasing any mental chatter. Breath by breath, your mind quiets. Breath by breath, you find yourself deepening into your center. Breath by breath, deep relaxation and calm are available to you. Breathing and deepening. Breathing and deepening into your home.

In this place of home, allow a present or past issue of pain, discouragement or worry to surface in your awareness. As you allow this issue to surface, you feel a loving presence right there with you. This presence listens to your pain, hears your pain, and holds a place of loving acceptance for you in this pain. This presence also offers you a gift of comfort. Perhaps it is a word or sound. Perhaps this gift is a touch. Perhaps the gift is an object or symbol. It may even be a prayer shawl like those made by Joyce. Whatever the gift is, you find it to be just perfect for you. You take time now with this gift of comfort. You allow yourself to rest in this comfort. You soak this comfort into your very bones and deep into your cells. This comfort bathes your body, mind and spirit. It is here, immersed in this comfort, that you remember that whatever happened or is happening now, that all is well and you are not alone.

Honoring your own pace and timing, you know when it is time to bring your awareness back to the present moment and the place where you began this meditation. You give gratitude for the comfort and know that you bring that very comfort back with you into your ordinary consciousness and everyday life. Should you need reminding of the comfort that is with you, remembering the gift given to you brings you right back in touch with that comfort.

When you are ready, you return now to the place where you began this meditation. You feel the structure of whatever is supporting your body. Your senses become aware of the place where you began, the sounds, the smells, the temperature and the felt sense of your skin. Taking a couple of comfortable breaths you now open your eyes, bringing comfort with you into your present environment. You take all the time you need to integrate your experience.

You may wish to share your experience with a friend or companion. You may also wish to journal about your experience.

THE DOORWAY OF THE BODY

How much and what kind of exercise do I need? What antioxidants are needed and which foods contain them? What anti-aging creams are available now? How many hours of sleep are optimal? Vitamins or no vitamins? Organic or non-organic? Gluten or gluten-free? We can be so inundated with questions like this that it can be overwhelming to tend this precious body.

Some of us perceive the body as a machine and focus on its muscles, organ systems and the movements we can make. Some cultures and spiritual traditions consider the body to be the temple of the spirit. Some of us see the body as having desires and needs that must be overcome. Some believe that the body itself is sacred. There are many ways we perceive our physical form.

I believe that all the aspects of self are connected. I like to view our wholeness as the integration of all our parts. I believe that body, mind, emotion and spirit (or whatever we name that larger perspective part of us) are woven together in a way that is often mysterious. In both the personal and professional parts of my life, I have had opportunities to see through the window that holds this mystery. Here I share some of those glimpses.

≈

Tally comes in to my office for a standard Swedish massage. She has been working extra hours at a demanding job in a small nearby town. She is also involved in community organizations, is a devoted wife and the mother of nine-year-old twins. She wants a massage to relieve some of the physical tension in her shoulders, neck and back. She has had massages before, but it has been awhile.

I start some soft music, at her request, and leave the room. Once she tells me she's ready, I enter and set my intention inside myself that I am in partnership with Tally's own inner healer and that every touch can offer her what is in her highest and best good.

I learn quickly that Tally is a good receiver. Her body meets each stroke and the muscles respond by softening and releasing places of tension. We are about half way through our time together and I begin a gentle rocking motion for her body. She begins to cry. At first, they are gentle, flowing tears. Then she begins to sob softly and her body shakes from the emotion.

I say simply, "If there are words with this emotion that you wish to speak aloud, they are welcome. And if not, that's okay too."

Tally begins to tell me that her twins, one boy and one girl, had been born prematurely and spent time in a neonatal intensive care unit. While all the medical people told her nothing she had done contributed to their early arrival, part of her still felt guilty and responsible. She told me that her twins were healthy and, in nine years had never suffered any ill effects of their early birth, and she thought she'd put the guilt behind her. But when I began that rocking motion with her body, she thought about the words from "Rock-a-Bye Baby," that well-known children's lullaby. Thinking about them somehow brought up the guilt that had been buried and she cried. I just held the space for her by remaining present inside myself as she moved through the big wave of emotion. There was nothing to fix or do. All that was needed was to honor her experience with silent witnessing and trust her to be with her own process. When the wave had passed, she wanted to verbally process her emotional response to that memory from nine years ago and so we did.

We brainstormed ways for her to honor the part of her that had carried that guilt and what it might need to release that guilt for good. Tally felt that she needed to write a letter to her twins, a letter she would never give them, explaining her guilt and apologizing for any way she had unintentionally contributed to their premature birth. She also wanted to express how very proud she was to be their mother and how she marveled at the miracle of their lives. In addition, Tally decided that she wanted to write a letter from her Wisdom Self to her guilty part offering forgiveness, even though she knew logically that none was needed. Still, she wanted to reassure that part that she was a wonderful mother and that all was well.

Tally returned a few weeks later and shared that she had followed through with those letters and that she felt freer than she had in some time. She had let go of something she hadn't even consciously known she was still carrying. As a result, she felt even closer to her husband and children. She felt lighter and knew she was carrying less tension in her body. She felt like she had more perspective in her work and that she was more balanced in her sense of responsibility there. She was still marveling at the mystery of how something as simple as rocking her body had opened the doorway to this healing. I am still marveling, too.

≈

Dressed in a three-piece suit, tie tight up at his neck, Ted came stiffly into my office. He presented as somewhat formal and distant, very businesslike as he told me of being the owner of his own successful company. His speech was short and clipped. Ted told me he suffered from chronic back pain and had come to me to for a different kind of bodywork after other kinds of healing modalities, Western and complementary alike, were unsuccessful. But he didn't want information. He just wanted to get on the massage table. He really didn't want to take time to do the medical history part. He didn't care how this healing worked. He didn't have any questions. He was in a hurry and wanted results, yesterday.

Often in my work, clients want to address the mind/body/spirit connection. When I met Ted that day I thought, *I hope I can help him with pain relief. We are going to be addressing just the body here. He has no interest is exploring anything other than the physicality of his pain. Don't even try to offer a larger perspective. He will have none of it.*

I'm a bit ashamed of it, but these were my biases.

We proceeded with the basic protocol of his requested bodywork. At the end, Ted thought he might have noticed some minor relief of his pain. He didn't really want to talk about it and was just ready to pay the fee, schedule another appointment (to my surprise), and leave. I took a deep breath and accommodated his wishes.

Before Ted arrived for his second appointment, I readied myself to be extra efficient and put on my professional body-worker hat. When he came in to my office, he sat down and said, "I have a question for you before we go to the table."

"Fine," I said. "Go ahead."

Ted looked me in the eye, making his first real connection. "What do you think about what our culture calls God?"

I could have fallen off my chair. Never would I have imagined that this would be happening. I smiled, noticed my heart softening toward Ted as I did so, and shared some things with him from my own perspective, making it clear that these were only my opinions and that I was happy to explore his opinions and beliefs, too. We spent that hour in spiritual direction or mentoring, and it was an amazing and inspirational hour. Ted shared how he had resisted giving voice to his deep questions of meaning and purpose, and how such pondering had made him uncomfortable until now. He didn't understand the logic of it, but something about touch had opened a place in him where he could give permission to voice and consider such things. Ted wasn't looking for simplistic answers, and I had none, but he was looking for a safe place to explore and wonder. That day was a beautiful example of the importance of that very thing.

Ted continued coming regularly for a few months and while we didn't focus on his back pain directly, he did tell me it had diminished significantly, though this wasn't the real gift of our connection. As is true of many of my clients, I felt like Ted was my teacher. He taught me to put away my preconceived notions. He taught me to notice my biases and then to let them go and open to the mystery, the possibilities beyond those biases. He reminded me of the power of the mind/body/spirit connection. He showed me in a dramatic way that the body can be a doorway through which we can access our deeper self. He helped me remember to be open to the unexpected. Those sessions with him are still teaching me.

I believe our bodies are impacted by heredity, our environment and especially how we are nurtured, by what we choose to eat and drink, and by injury, accidents and how we process information and experiences. Our bodies are also impacted by the wisdom, memory, story and mystery that can't always be explained and understood but that is carried within each—and all—of us. I believe we are all connected. I believe that my body, mind, emotion and spirit are all woven into my wholeness. When my wholeness connects with yours, we get glimpses of the wondrously unexpected. It is my intention to remain open to those magical places, the places of wisdom through the doorway of the body.

Reflection Questions and Journal Prompts

- *What, if anything, do these stories touch in you?*

- *What is your perspective of the human body?*

- *Have you ever had an experience like Tally or Ted?*

- *What experiences in your own life might remind you that your body, mind, emotion, and spirit are connected?*

- *Do you notice physical issues in your body that you suspect might be related to an emotional, cognitive or spiritual issue that is working on you or may be incomplete?*

- *Are you listening to or acting on your intuition about any incomplete issues? If so, what have you found as the best fit for you? If not, what might you consider exploring?*

Suggested Activities or Experiences

- *If you are having a body issue that your intuition tells you may be related to more than a physical issue, you might consider talking with that body part. For example, if your knee has been a concern, you might first talk to your knee, offer empathy, ask if there is something it needs that is isn't getting and if there is something it is trying to tell you. Then you allow a time of quiet so you can hear what it might have to say. You can talk to your body aloud or in writing to it and letting it write back to you.*

- *You might sculpt your body using clay. If there is an area of your body that you are working with you might pay particular attention to the sculpting of that part. You could also incorporate body dialogue here, as well. In body dialogue you speak to your knee, for example, and then let it speak back to you. The dialogue can go back and forth as long as it seems to flow for us. We can do this verbally or by writing. We may be surprised at what our body tells us it needs in order to return to harmony or health.*

- *You might pick an appropriate piece of music and do a dance or movement for that body part, or as that body part, and be open to its communication in this way.*

- *You may be called to try a new kind of bodywork or healing modality with the intention of allowing your body to open up its communication with you or tell you its story.*

- *You could touch that part of your body and intend sending it the energy of healing on all levels.*

Meditation on Communicating with Your Body

Begin by finding a comfortable place to sit or lie down where you won't be disturbed. Close your eyes if that is comfortable for you. Allow your awareness to come to your breath. For now, just notice the breath. In and out, in and out. Let the breath breathe you. Be breathed by the breath. Take all the time you need right now to just be with the breath.

And when you are ready, you welcome your body into this day, into this experience. Begin by bringing loving awareness to the body. Just notice the body and how it is at this moment of this day. There is no need to change anything and there is no judgment, only loving awareness of the body. Notice any places of tension, discomfort or holding. Notice any places of ease, flow and comfort in the body. Welcome the body into this experience, this day and breathe a breath of acceptance to the body. Only after extending awareness, welcome and acceptance to the body do you notice if there is any tension, holding or energy in the body, that is no longer needed, that is ready to be released. If so, then you just let it go, perhaps sailing it out on the exhaled breath. And if this created any new spaciousness in the body, you can use your breath to expand out the health and wholeness that lives at your core into this newly opened space. You may also breathe in the wholeness energy available in the larger universe outside of you. Breathing in, and expanding out health and wholeness for the body.

You can extend this same welcome to the emotion self. Begin by noticing with loving awareness whatever emotions are present with you this moment of this day. No judgment, no right or wrong, no need to change anything. For now, just notice the emotion self. Welcome the emotion self into this day. When you are ready, breathe a breath of acceptance to the emotion self no matter what is found there. And only after this welcoming and this extending of acceptance, notice if there is any emotion energy that is no longer needed that is ready to be released. If there is, just let it go. No forcing, no effort, just releasing. Perhaps you send it out with the support of the exhaled breath. Release it in whatever is your way. And if this has created any new spaciousness in your emotion self, you expand out the emotional health and wholeness that lives at your core into this newly opened space. You may also wish to partner this with breathing in the larger emotion health and wholeness energy available from the larger universe outside of you. Breathe in and expand out to fill the emotion self with health and wholeness.

You can give this same gift now to your thinking mind. Take time to pause and notice with loving awareness the thoughts and beliefs moving through the mind along with any mental chatter present at this moment of this day. Pause to notice the thoughts without the need to engage them and perhaps remember that the thoughts are not necessarily your deeper truths. After a few moments of noticing, you welcome your thinking mind into this day and this experience. Breathe a breath of acceptance to your mind. And only after noticing, welcoming and extending acceptance, do you notice if there are any old beliefs that are no longer true for you or any mental chatter or thoughts that are no longer needed. If there are, and they are ready to be released, just let them go. Do this with the support of your exhaled breath or whatever is your way. And if this creates any new spaciousness in your mind, expand out the peace and wholeness that lives at your core to fill this space. Again, you may wish to partner this with the peace and harmony that also lives in the world outside of you. Breathe in and expand out to cultivate peace and harmony for the mind.

Now, you have created an environment where your wisest Self can emerge. And so you pause and breathe and be as this Self that is your true nature. You take all the time you need deepening your connection as this wise and expansive Self.

This may be the place of completion of this meditation for you. You may just rest in this place until you feel complete and then return to your ordinary consciousness and the place you first began this meditation.

However, you may in your imagination go on a journey of deepening your communication with your body. If you say "yes" to this journey, you make an inner commitment to explore and suspend judgment and release any preset expectations.

When you are ready you allow yourself to travel in your imagination to a safe place and a place that feels special to you. It may be a place you have actually been or a new place altogether. Trust yourself to know the perfect place for you.

As you arrive in this special place you notice the sights, sounds, physical sensations and any other awareness. You allow yourself to soak up the beauty, safety and specialness of this place. When you are ready, you notice a loving presence, helper or guide who is approaching you. You feel only love and unconditional acceptance from this helper. As the helper stands before you, you understand that your helper is willing to guide you to a special place for your body to open itself in deeper communication with you. You say a comfortable "yes" and before long, you and your helper have found that special place for your body to open itself to you. You open to any initial ceremony or process that helps your body get ready. You trust yourself and your helper so that this unfolds in a way that is just right for you.

When the preparations have been completed your helper encourages you to find the right place to sit or lie down. You are asked to breathe comfortably and to intend that each breath help soften and open the doorway of the body so that it might communicate in a deeper way with you. Softening and opening, softening and opening. Perhaps gradually, perhaps all at once your body opens in a way that feels new or deeper for you. In this opening it begins to share in a way that offers you a more intimate connection with it. You receive whatever amount or kind of sharing is offered as if you are communicating with your oldest and dearest friend.

When you are ready you thank your body for all it has shared and you and your guide begin the journey back to where you began. You thank your guide and know that you can return and repeat this or a similar experience any time you wish.

Now you are ready to bring your awareness back to ordinary consciousness. Allow a couple of deep breaths. Begin to feel the surface of whatever has been supporting your body during this meditation. Notice any sounds or fragrances in the place where this meditation began. And when you are ready, you open your eyes and allow all the time you need to reorient to this time and place, to this present moment.

You may wish to share your experience with a friend or companion. Perhaps you may want to journal.

SACRED SPACES

Sacred spaces can run the gamut from the simple to the extraordinary but regardless of what they look like, or where they are found, they can all offer the same wondrous thing. When we hear the words "sacred space" in our culture we immediately think of cathedrals and churches, ashrams, temples, mosques and other particular places created for members of commonly known spiritual traditions to worship.

When I think of sacred space, I think of a place free of judgment and criticism, a place that welcomes and accepts, a place of inspiration that touches the place in us that yearns to be the very best we can be, a place that helps us to access that which is sacred and holy in ourselves. Sacred spaces invite us into a connection with what author Michael Morwood calls the Everywhere Presence, which is also known by many other names, including God, Buddha, Allah, Creator, Great Spirit, Goddess, Atman, the Holy, Divine Presence, Sophia and Holy Breath, just to name a few. No matter what language feels right to us, sacred space then can assist us in knowing the holy that is both inside of us and all around us and offer us a place to join in community with the holy in others.

As a child, I was fortunate to know many sacred spaces. I knew sacred space for a few years in the local church to which my family belonged. I felt a sense of community there with my extended family, friends, classmates and neighbors from my small town. I felt the something-larger-than-me, then named as God in that church. I couldn't have given voice to it then, but I also felt there that goodness in me, that spark of the Holy that lives in me.

Another structure that offered me the same sense of sacred connection included the old brooder house, essentially an old chicken house that my parents lovingly cleaned up and transformed into a playhouse. It was here that I spent nearly every free waking hour during the warmer months. In the same way the fragrance of incense, the presence of statues and hymnal songs, and hard pews were part of the sacred space of my childhood church; the spark of the Holy was experienced sitting at those old refinished school desks, organizing the kitchen items handed down by my mother on those shelves built by my busy farmer father. I felt at home with the creak, creak, creak of the old discarded rocking chair by the windows draped with the curtains hand-made by my mother who struggled to sew. This brooder house was also place where I could feel a sense of inner and outer "home."

The river was another place that held me and comforted me when I needed to be reminded of the bigger sense of things within and all around me. I would walk or ride my bike down the old dirt road, past the corn, bean or hay fields to the riverbank where I would sit for hours watching the river flow. The comfort I found there during adolescence and other times of angst, like when my grandfather died, was immeasurable. The flow of that river reminded me that there is a flow to life that can carry us beyond our suffering into the next chapter of our life.

I received comfort and acceptance sitting on that riverbank amidst the song of the cottonwood leaves dancing on their branches, I felt at home inside myself. I also felt something larger, something of that Everywhere Presence holding me in a way that told me I belonged here, too. Throughout my childhood, sacred spaces were places of solitude but they could also be shared with others, too. What all of them—my small-town church, the brooder house, the river—had in common was an offering of acceptance, a reminder of something larger than my individual self, a holding of me in celebration, sorrow, anger and change. They moved me past feeling stuck where I was to the next place in the unfolding of my life.

As an adult, I have found sacred space by the ocean and gulf, in the desert and tropics, in cabins, retreat centers and fine hotels. With the aging of my mom, my sister has created a sacred space for family to gather on most holidays. I have found sacred space in solitude and with others, in churches, temples, meeting houses and classrooms. I have felt it sitting in stillness, moving in dances of universal peace, walking with nature spirits, and in rest. I have come to it at my table of sacred, special touchstone objects and through sacred texts and inspirational reading. I have heard it in a wide range of music and in some of the last breaths of my father before his death in this world. It has appeared in intentionally set sacred space and spontaneously when I have been present to the experience offered to me. Now, if I could just sense it when I iron, clean my oven and shoo away mosquitos. That hasn't happened yet, though it has been my experience that the Holy can find us in all ways and in all places.

In my work, I often invite those I am honored to be with to begin our time together by consciously entering into co-creative sacred space. I invite that we each, in our own way, welcome and bring all of who we are into our time together. I encourage that we invite not only our human self aspects (body, emotion, small mind, inner child, critic, to name a few); I also encourage us to invite the most Expansive Self, whether we call it our Divine Spark, Higher Self, Christ Light, Buddha Nature, Large Mind or Higher Consciousness.

This Higher Self *is* the sacred space inside of us. When this inner sacred space comes into relationship with the inner sacred space of another, perhaps in an external sacred space, wondrous things can and do happen. Those wondrous things are born from a climate of belonging, of setting aside judgment and criticism, and instead calling forth the energies of acceptance that open us to inspiration and possibility.

Whether we are experiencing sacred space inside ourselves, with another or in an external setting, it is here we can explore, question, claim, process, grow, change and transform. Sacred space, both inner and outer, can hold us until we can move beyond current suffering and harvest whatever gifts may be found in that suffering. Sacred space– whether in an office, a church, temple, mosque, by the river, in an old chicken house, or inside ourselves–invites us to something more and welcomes us to where home *is* "home."

Reflection Questions and Journal Prompts

- *What thoughts, feelings or memories come up for you in reading this section?*

- *As you reflect back on your childhood, did you have sacred places that held you? If so, how would you describe them?*

- *Were your childhood sacred places ones of solitude or community, or a mixture of each?*

- *What stories can you share about your childhood times in sacred space?*

- *As an adult, where have you found sacred space, and with whom? Have these places been intentionally sought out or happened upon? Have these experiences been in solitude? In community?*

- *Are there places where you connect with your own inner sacred space, you own inner divinity?*

- *How might you describe the experience of being in your own inner sense of sacred space or your inner spiritual home?*

- *How might an ordinary place or experience be transformed into one of sacred space felt inside or around you? Can you share stories of this from your life?*

Suggested Activities or Experiences

- *If it is not already your practice to do so, you might wish to find time to be consciously in a sacred space. Just notice how this is for you.*

- *Imagine moving through an entire day as if you are in sacred space. If you forget, just notice with loving awareness and return to the sense of being all day in a sacred space.*

- *Imagine moving through an entire day as if you ARE sacred space, as if everywhere you go is made more sacred by your bringing your own Sacred Self there.*

- *Is there music, poetry, readings, or movement that speaks to you of sacred space? You may wish to incorporate this into your life even more frequently.*

Meditation on Sacred Space

Begin by finding a place to sit or lie down for this meditation where you won't be disturbed. Take a couple of comfortable deep breaths. Allow yourself to spend a few minutes just breathing and noticing your breath.

When you are ready, allow yourself to imagine going somewhere that is a sacred place for you. This may be a place that you have visited, somewhere in your own home, or a place you imagine. Trust yourself to journey in your imagination to the perfect place. In this place, notice what there is to see around you. Notice what fragrances are present. Notice any tastes. Notice the sounds present here. Notice all the physical sensations. Notice that everything there for your five senses is just right for you.

As you take time to relax into this place, notice how it is here for your body. Notice how it is here for your emotion self. Notice how it is here for your thinking mind. And notice how you are aware of that something in you that is larger than your personality or ego self. Just notice with loving awareness. As you sink into this place of your Expansive Self, if you haven't already, invite or consciously welcome the Everywhere Presence that is that Expansive Self and is also beyond that expansive Self. Notice how this Presence makes itself known to you in just the perfect way for you. Notice your joining with this Larger Presence.

In the sacredness of this place, settle into this experience and sink into "being." Here there is nothing to do. Here there is nothing to earn. Here there is only now, this moment. Here there is only love and peace. Here you take all the time you need.

When you are ready, honoring your own pace and timing, prepare to leave this place and return to ordinary consciousness. As you ready to leave, take a moment to breathe this experience into your very bones. You breathe it into every cell. You breathe it into your deepest memory places. You have entered the experience of this sacred place and it has entered you. There is no separation. And so as you return, you are bringing all the gifts and the felt sense of this time into your ordinary life. You invite this sacred space to go with you into the next chapter of your day, into all your days.

Take a couple of comfortably deep breaths now. Feel the structure of the surface that supports you as you return to the place where you first began this meditation. Notice the sounds in that place. Notice the temperature there. As you are ready you open your eyes. You give thanks for the experience and enter the next part of your day when you are ready.

You may wish to journal about your experience or share it with a friend or companion.

A LABYRINTH WALK WITH AN UNLIKELY GUIDE

Stretches of dark, cloudy days, mounds of frozen snow and ice, slippery roads, and temperatures with below-zero wind chills can wear me out. The sun has always been good medicine for my soul, and even the briefest time in the desert Southwest is a good place for me to find that medicine.

With the large blue sky, sun sparkling on abundant nature, walking trails, and a hermitage for solitude, this retreat center was the perfect place for rest and replenishment. There were lots of places for prayer and quiet, reading and contemplation. I could be in complete solitude or with other retreat guests in silence or conversation. The fact that the dining room offered state of the art healthy food didn't hurt either. I was in heaven.

The hermitage was lovely, and I smiled as I read the guest information detailing all there was to offer. The section alerting guests about the local wildlife and appropriate caution in the case of a wildlife encounter was particularly interesting. I read about scorpions, roadrunners, bobcats, javelina (a new one for me), coyote, rattlesnakes, lizards, toads, and other desert life. I read about who to avert your gaze with, who to stare at, who to back away from, who to stand your ground with and so on. "It's nice to be among things not so frozen they can't move," I thought. Still, I was uncertain I would ever need to know all this. True, I'd heard one of the cooks tell about throwing a chair at a javelina that acted as if it were going to charge at him. He said a javelina resembles a big pig or boar, with the addition of a bristle-like rise on the head. He also said one needed to be cautious around them because they travel in family groups. I was feeling thankful that my only encounters with the wildlife had been the gift of a bobcat sighting.

My retreats begin with an initial "downshifting" from the hectic, busy pace of life that often draws me in, regardless of my daily spiritual practice. My pace slowed, I walked more slowly and mindfully, I breathed deeper and more fully, I was present in a way that could allow a real appreciation of all creation, gratitude for life, and the constant awareness of the Presence within and all around me.

Ordinarily, I don't connect with the outer world back home while I am on retreat because it seems to go against all the downshifting I have done. But one morning I awoke with the nagging sense that something wasn't right with one of my spiritual direction clients. I sat with this in my centering time and knew I needed to explore this a bit more. So I called my office voice mail and, sure enough, there was a message from this client's partner that he was in the hospital and was not expected to live. Struggles with a chronic health issue had been depleting his energy, and now he seemed to be giving up. He'd previously spoken to me of having times where he just wished it were his time to go, to die. Lately he hadn't been any more ill than usual so it was a surprise to everyone that he seemed to be deteriorating so fast. It was clear that going home wouldn't change anything and so the question became, *"What can I do to offer support from here?"*

Praying in the chapel and lighting a candle for him was a given, and this I did. As I did so, I became aware that I needed to walk the outdoor labyrinth on the property for him. So that evening after dinner, I carried my backpack, a journal, and water and went behind all of the buildings to the grounds' outdoor labyrinth. I sat on the bench near the labyrinth entrance and centered myself amidst the gentle breeze, the cacti, and desert flora. There was no one else around and I felt comfort in the solitude.

Sitting there in the quiet, I noticed the lowering sun casting its luminous glow on the beautiful reddish-colored desert stone that outlined the labyrinth path in the sandy earth. I reviewed what I knew of the labyrinth as an ancient spiritual and meditative tool. Following the winding path can bring a sense of calm, clarity, and connection with a deep knowing and the reminder that we are not alone in this life; that a great Presence is with us. Walking this winding path is like a pilgrimage. We set out in order to go within. Walking the labyrinth is a metaphor for our journey of life, one moment, one chapter, or our life as a whole. What we encounter along the way is a metaphor for what is going on in our life. For example, if we think we will never reach the center it can remind us that life can seem pretty long sometimes, like we will never reach our destination or goal. But in the labyrinth, as in life, we find that if we just keep going, we will find our way. Though the labyrinth can look like a maze, there are no tricks or dead ends; there is only one continuous path that winds to the center and back out again.

During those few minutes on the bench, before I began, I decided that I would dedicate this walk to my client. I would walk this path for him, as if he were walking it himself. I offered my intention for each of the three stages of the walk on behalf of my client. I would dedicate the walk, as it wound from the entrance and into the center, to letting go and releasing for my client anything that was no longer needed or that impeded his journey. I would pause in the center to listen for wisdom, guidance or to simply be with the Holy. And finally, I would leave the center and wind my way back and forth toward the place I began, carrying any new insights and a willingness to bring the gifts received back out into the world on his behalf. I would walk knowing that the path we begin is never the same as the one on which we return. I felt that while my client wasn't a religious person, and I wasn't even sure he knew what a labyrinth was; his deep sense of spirituality would resonate on some level with this kind of prayer.

I believe that walking this type of sacred path can connect us to the Oneness and the collective consciousness, and I hoped that perhaps on some level he would sense, feel, or know the wisdom of this journey as if he were the one placing step after step upon the path. I hoped it would bring him healing in whatever way would serve him in life or in death.

I entered the labyrinth. My steps were slow, sometimes halting and I had a sense that my feet were really no longer *my* feet; they were borrowed feet. The journey in continued in a slow manner as if there was much that was willingly released and surrendered into a greater Presence. Back and forth, back and forth, short straight-aways and turns, longer straight-aways and more turns, and after what seemed like a very long time, I arrived in the center. A large boulder became a resting place there, and I went into a meditative space to offer a connection with the Holy. At first, I was aware my thoughts were restless before they gradually settled. Time passed, but I have no idea how long, and then I felt such a deep, deep, trusting peace that it brought tears to my eyes. The Holy was making Itself known and there were no words; there was no space or time.

At last it became clear that it was time to leave the center and wind back to where I began, all the while carrying the gifts given willingly out into the world on my client's behalf. I had only taken a few steps out from the center when I heard a loud rustling from the desert brush on the left. Into full view lumbered a very large, scary looking creature. *"Could it be? It must be. Holy cow. It is. It's a javelina,"* I realized. Indeed, it sported a very bristly-looking Mohawk-like thing on its head. It was intensely muscular and only a few feet away from me. It looked big, it looked mean, and I was afraid. My heart was pumping wildly and my mind was racing to remember, *"Is this the one I stand still for? Am I supposed to avert my gaze? Stare at it? Back away? What am I supposed to do?"*

I wish I could say that I stood still because I wisely remembered that is what one is supposed to do when coming upon a javelina. But, honestly, I froze from sheer fright, not any sense of wisdom. I averted my gaze. I looked around for help. There was no one there, and I remembered they travel in family groups. *Where were the rest of them? How many were there?* I worried and I listened, expecting the others to join from the brush. I had no patio chair to throw at them, and could do nothing but pray. Pounding, pounding, pounding. My heart felt like it was beating outside my chest. What seemed like hours passed, exhausting hours. Then, the javelina, all by itself, no family group in sight, lumbered across the clearing and into the brush on the other side from where it came.

I am so afraid and there is not much light left now in the day. I really, really just want to take off and *run* back to my hermitage. But a part of me has the sense to check in. *"Is it the highest good to just leave without completing the labyrinth walk, or do I persevere and finish the walk in spite of my fear?"* Somehow I knew I needed to finish the walk. I realized, on some level, that this is what the journey was about: finish the walk, finish the journey; don't let fear keep you from completion. Perhaps this was symbolic for me, perhaps for my client. I didn't need to know. I just walked. I walked afraid. I walked with my pounding heart. I walked with weak knees and shallow breath. I walked. I walked. I walked. I walked with heightened awareness. I kept going in spite of my fear. I kept going though it seemed as if it might take forever. And as I walked I calmed. My heart stopped racing, my breathing deepened, and a sense of lightness and joy arrived. I felt like laughing, and I did. As I exited the labyrinth, I turned and bowed to the teachings given me and trusted that whatever was happening with my client was just right, divinely guided.

And yet . . . did I pause at the bench to journal? No way! I gathered my backpack and my journal and got myself back to my hermitage. The journaling could happen there!

As I journaled, I questioned: *"Was this walk really for my client? Was it for me? Was it for both of us?"* I didn't know, and released the need to know. What I felt sure of was that something powerful had been released. A powerful peace and sense of the Holy being present had been felt. And fear had arisen, big fear. The crucial question was, *"Do I stop when I am afraid or do I keep going?"*

I found that I could pause and then keep going in spite of fear. And I learned that it was empowering to feel that joy and lightness and hear the laughter on the other side of fear.

No other voice mails were in my box those next few days. Within a week of my return home, I had a call from my client's partner. My client, out of the hospital, was making a remarkable recovery. He wanted to see me. When we met, I shared with him the story of the labyrinth. He was grateful and could see how the walk had paralleled his story. While unconscious and sedated, he'd had an inner journey, his own labyrinth walk of sorts. He had released some baggage, old beliefs and perceptions. Though he was afraid of a life of struggle and suffering, he made a renewed commitment to live his life, to complete whatever it was he was called here for.

A few years have passed and this man is now more dynamic and healthy. He is committed to life and living it with gusto and a kind of vibrancy. He still questions. He is a dedicated spiritual journeyer. He is still listening to discern how he is to make a difference in our world. He now knows that though he had often wished for death, he wasn't done, it wasn't his time. He remains a gift to our world.

What role the labyrinth walk played in all this will remain a part of the sacred mystery. What unexpected guides will accompany us on our life journey also remains a mystery. Who's next? Scorpions? Lizards? Roadrunners?

The journey continues.

Reflection Questions or Journal Prompts

- *What stands out or touches you from this story?*

- *Are you aware of times of needing to downshift from the busyness of your life?*

- *What places, practices or activities can assist you in that downshifting?*

- *What might be signs of successful downshifting in your life?*

- *Can you share experiences of your intuition speaking to you?*

- *Sometimes we may need to stand our ground or move through fear. Sometimes fear is an indicator to stop or move away. How do you discern what fear is telling you? Can you share some examples of each from your life?*

- *If you ever find yourself yearning for minutes, hours or even days of retreat time, what kind of retreat time would offer you rest and replenishment? Would you consider at least an overnight retreat? Why? Why not?*

- *Have you walked a labyrinth? Where can you go to walk one if this appeals to you?*

- *What ways do you have of releasing or shedding old thoughts, old beliefs, old experiences or situations that are no longer needed in your life? Is there something you're ready to let go of currently? If so, how might you do that?*

- *What ways do you have of coming to your own center and/or a larger sense of the Center? How does this centering serve or support you in your life?*

- *Do you have some awareness of the gifts and talents that come into this world through you? What are some of those gifts?*

- *How do you find yourself bringing those unique gifts and talents into our world?*

Retreat Time Meditation

Sit or lie down in a place where you can be comfortable and away from any interruptions. Taking time to center a bit, just notice how your body is in this moment. No judgment, no need to change anything, just notice with loving awareness.

Briefly pause . . .

Welcome your body just as it is into this day. Only after this welcoming of your body, do you notice if there is any energy in the body that is no longer needed that is ready to be released. If there is, just let it go, perhaps with the support of your exhaled breath. If there is any new spaciousness in your body as a result of this releasing, just expand out into this space the wholeness that lives at your core.

Now just notice how it is with your emotion self. With loving awareness, just notice the mixture of emotions present. Beyond the place where we have learned to label emotions as good or bad, just notice.

Briefly pause . . .

Welcome whatever you find in this part of you that carries and experiences emotion. Only after the welcoming you notice if there is any emotion energy that is no longer needed that is ready to be released. If there is, just allow that release. No need to force. No need to effort. Just allow that release, again perhaps with the support of your exhaled breath. Just allow that energy to move out into the larger universe to be transformed. And if this results in any new spaciousness within you, just expand out the emotional wholeness that lives at your core into this newly opened space.

Now give this same gift of noticing to your thinking mind. Allow yourself to pause and just notice from a place of loving detachment. Notice any mental chatter, any thoughts and beliefs moving through. Here, we can remember that our thoughts are not necessarily our deeper truth.

Briefly pause . . .

Now welcome all that you find in the thinking mind. Only after this welcoming do you notice if there is any mental chatter, any old beliefs or thoughts that no longer serve you. If they are ready to be released, simply allow their release, with the help of the exhaled breath or whatever release feels right to you.

If you now have any new spaciousness in the thinking mind, allow the peace of mind that lives at your core to expand out and fill this space, bringing more peace of mind.

You have now welcomed the body, the emotion self and the thinking mind into this moment. The way has been made clear to reconnect, once again, with your wisdom self; your High Self, your intuitive self, your spirit. Use the language that is just right for you.

Rest for a few quiet moments now in this expansive place of your true nature, your essence, your Big Picture Self. Breathe and rest. Breathe and rest.

From this expansive Self, imagine now that you can walk into a perfect retreat space designed just for you. Enter this place at your own pace. Just notice what surrounds you. Are you indoors or outside? Are you alone or with others? What colors or images draw your attention? What things are there to enhance a time of rest and nurturing for you? What is the temperature? What does your skin notice? What sounds gift your ears? What tastes might you savor? What scents are there? Just pause in luxurious spaciousness to take it all in. Linger where you are called to linger. Experience what you are called to experience. Be, breathe and rest in this special retreat just for you.

When it is time to move from this place you notice that you are taking with you a word, a symbol, or some reminder of this place. Whatever you are taking with you, reminds you of the gifts of this time. It reminds you that you can return here any time you need to rest or be restored.

Carrying your reminder with you, you now slowly and at your own pace return your consciousness to the place where you originally sat or lay down to enter this meditation. You breathe and open your eyes when you are ready. And honoring your own pace and timing, you bring whatever gifts and blessings from your retreat time with you into the next chapter of your day.

You may wish to journal, draw or otherwise express your experience.

THE LAND OF SORROW

It was oh so dark, cold, and damp. The most ordinary day, the most innocent moment can open into a land where there is no GPS, no familiar routes to follow. We resist going there but we cannot say no. What we find there and whom we find there can be quite surprising.

November 2001 contained that ordinary day opening then into a new land, when my father was diagnosed with small cell carcinoma–an aggressive, terminal, type of lung cancer. While I have always considered myself a spiritual person, my greatest fear had always been the death of my father and I felt myself being pulled into this new land of profound sorrow.

Dad and I had closeness, a heart connection that cannot be explained with words. You may have experienced people in your life where it seems as if you have known them for all eternity. There is a familiarity of spirit even though you may not know their personality or human self. This was how it was for me with Dad. My first life memory was of being overjoyed that I could cuddle with the man who was always busy working, day and night, to support our family. He had the mumps and was forced to stop moving, stop working and made to rest. This four-year-old girl, not about to miss this opportunity, crawled right up on that couch and hunkered in.

Over the years we grew to know each other's human selves. I was able to know him beyond the hard work ethic. I admired his commitment to family, community, and church. I loved his sense of humor and the bantering back and forth that sharpened my mental jousting skills. He had good relationships, perhaps because he knew how to forgive. He was kind and a "glass-half-full" person. His deep love was often quietly expressed, like when he tucked my developmentally disabled aunt's doll into her casket at the last moment before the lid was lowered, or when he would fill the fireplace with wood before I came for a weekend visit because he knew I loved a roaring fire. I like to think he also grew from getting to know me. He quit littering after I asked him if he would throw garbage on his mother, then explaining how the Earth *is* the Mother for the Native Americans. He went from distant A-Frame hugs to full-bodied ones after years of me drawing him closer. He stopped telling off-color, distasteful jokes (at least to me) after numerous pleas. He eventually risked saying aloud, "I love you," and moved to some level of comfort with the expression of emotion.

I didn't know if my heart could take the pain of being separated from him and the stable, wise anchor he was for me. No amount of spiritual evolution, intellectualization, denial, or well-intended advice giving was going to get me a pass out of this land of sorrow. There would be no escape from the tough questions. "*How could I possibly navigate such sorrow? Could I journey with him through illness? Could I be present with the suffering, pain and heartache? Could I travel to the depths of my own sorrow and still have a loving, open heart available to offer understanding, compassion, love and support? Would the death of one so close change the very nature of who I am? Would it alter the way I am in the world? Would my sense of Spirit, a loving Presence be changed?*"

Always a crier, I cried buckets. My heart ached in a way that I found myself holding my chest from the pain within my body, mind and spirit. In those first few days after his diagnosis, I was comforted by the reminder of the Chinese kanji character for the word "crisis." The translation contains both the word "danger" and "opportunity." I realized, that if I were to survive this land of sorrow, I had to use this time as opportunity. So I began to learn all I could about Dad's cancer, its treatment, and his treatment team. It was good to have information journeying with me in that sorrow.

But even more than focusing on the medical information piece, I took the opportunity to be, really *be* present with him, in every moment I could, whether it was in person or on the phone. When Dad asked me to sit down with him as he wrote his own obituary, I felt the steady strength of Divine Presence through my tears.

Presence cleared the way for me to have intimate conversations with Dad as he relived his memory of a near death experience 10 years earlier during the placement of a pacemaker. He found himself in a "vortex of light" that was loving, calm and peaceful and he was unafraid. He said he was sent back because it wasn't his time. And you'd have to know my dad to know that "vortex of light" wasn't a familiar phrase. He waited two years to tell about this, and only then to a couple of us, because he thought we'd think him crazy. Because of this experience he knew there was something grand waiting for him and he wasn't afraid to die. He shared his worries about Mom and elicited a promise to take care of her, saying he hated to leave all of us. As he spoke, I felt light growing amidst the sorrow and the darkness. How could Divine Presence not be felt in this?

The biggest opportunity of all was to notice how Divine Presence was revealing itself through others in this land of sorrow.

Sister Marianne, while small in stature, brought big Presence and wise, deep eyes to us on the first frightening day at the Cancer Center when she met with our family offering hope and permission for tears, which I, in particular, loved. And she and Dad became good hug partners. "That Sister Marianne, she's a peach," he would say after her small acts of kindness and big acts of encouragement. She also helped my family navigate the sometimes-complex medical system and offered such practical wisdom as which hospital rooms had the best window views. More than a chaplain to us, we witnessed Divine Presence as it worked repeatedly through Sr. Marianne.

I felt Divine Presence there in my devoted mother, side by side, with my dad every exhausting step of the way. Through hospital stays, daily trips to the Cancer Center, reclaiming her driving skills, learning more medical information than imaginable, offering endless love, support and compassion, she was there.

Divine Presence lived through both my brothers and my sister as they gave many hours accompanying my parents to appointments and treatment sessions, tending to Mom and Dad's acreage and household, overnight stays in the hospital, numerous phone calls and balancing their own work with these things.

The establishing of a Do Not Resuscitate Order was grueling emotional work, but the guidance of the family doctor and many caring nurses brought great love into that process too.

More light in the darkness of sorrow was found, in my dad's humor, courage and wit that were still present with him in his final weeks and days. I was honored when he crowned me with the title of "Ornery Butt II" after a nurse had lovingly entitled him "Ornery Butt."

Eleven months after diagnosis, Divine Presence on the earth came marching through the hospital corridors, the phone connections, the mail, prayer lines, our family home and ultimately the church aisles at the funeral and visitation, in the form of countless friends and family. I'll never forget the love and sacrifice of some friends driving several hours to be present at Dad's vigil or service in spite of their own harvest, work schedule or likely desire to celebrate their birthday in a way other than being at a funeral visitation.

I also knew Divine Presence through Father Don, the local parish priest. He brought comfort during a communion and prayer visit to my parent's home. His hospital calls meant so much to all of us, and I was deeply moved and honored to have witnessed the final blessing he bestowed on my father in this life, where we shared in the words of that last Lord's Prayer. He guided us through the planning for the funeral and service details. His sermon about farming had me rethinking the spiritual farming nature of my own life work. And only the steadying of Divine Presence enabled me to read a tribute to my dad at his memorial visitation service.

I *am* different now. Navigating the dark, cold and unfamiliar places calls for both honoring the pain and being willing to look, when we can, with a broader vision for the gifts alongside the suffering. Traveling through the land of sorrow initially did feel like danger and yet there truly were opportunities. I think I'm more real, like the Velveteen Rabbit whom love transformed. I'm definitely more worn. I have faced my worst fear and navigated through unfamiliar and dark terrain. This kind of journeying has me claiming more courage in myself. I know now that I can journey with a loved one through life, death and rebirth. I have been gifted with the knowledge that I can be present to the deepest suffering, sorrow and pain. I now know that traveling to the deepest part of my own sorrow enables me to travel to deeper joy, intimacy, and celebration of life. This truth, which before lived in me as an idea or thought, now lives in me as a real experience. Seeing my father's death close up *has* changed me. I trust more; my life is richer. I am perhaps even more openhearted; I am now more available to do what I came here to this planet to do. I am now able to be even more a presence of love with others as they journey through *their* deepest sorrows and cultivate that same heart space for deep joy.

I have known Divine Presence in countless ways through my father's life, and then through the honor of journeying with him to his death. I have been gifted with Divine Presence in the voices, embraces, glances, words and actions of ordinary people. What a privilege to be on this journey of life. These experiences and memories will always live within me. May they support me in being that ordinary presence of Divine for those whose lives I touch.

I am grateful. Thank you, Dad.

Reflection Questions and Journal Prompts

- *What, if anything, resonates for you in this story?*

- *What are your own stories of sorrow or loss? What are your stories of navigating in a dark, unfamiliar place?*

- *What did you learn about yourself and others through those times? What helped you in the journey?*

- *What would you say were the "crises and opportunities" of those times?*

- *As you reflect back on times of deep sorrow and loss, could you see, sense or know Divine Presence?*

- *How did you tend yourself during these times?*

- *How have these experiences changed you?*

- *How have you, or are you, weaving these memories experiences into your life?*

Suggested Activities or Experiences

- *Perhaps you feel called to write one of your own stories of sorrow in narrative form or poetry.*

- *Perhaps you will do a dance of a sorrow, of its gifts and challenges.*

- *Perhaps there is a sculpture, painting, collage or drawing of sorrow waiting to come through you.*

- *Perhaps you would like to share a story of sorrow with a friend or companion.*

Meditation with Sorrow

Begin by finding a comfortable place to sit or lie down where you won't be disturbed. Allow your awareness to come to your breath. For now, just notice the breath. In and out, in and out. Let the breath breathe you. Be breathed by the breath. Take all the time you need right now to just be with the breath.

And when you are ready, you welcome your body into this day, into this experience. Begin by bringing loving awareness to the body. Just notice the body and how it is at this moment of this day. There is no need to change anything and there is no judgment, only loving awareness of the body. Notice any places of tension, discomfort or holding. Notice any places of ease, flow and comfort in the body. Welcome the body into this experience, this day and breathe a breath of acceptance to the body. Only after extending awareness, welcome and acceptance to the body do you notice if there is any tension, holding or energy in the body, that is no longer needed, that is ready to be released. If so, then you just let it go, perhaps sailing it out on the exhaled breath. And if this created any new spaciousness in the body, you can use your breath to expand out the health and wholeness that lives at your core into this newly opened space. You may also wish to partner that with breathing in the wholeness energy available in the larger universe outside of you. Breathing in, and expanding out health and wholeness for the body.

You can extend this same welcome to the emotion self. Begin by noticing with loving awareness whatever emotions are present with you this moment of this day. No judgment, no right or wrong, no need to change anything. For now just notice the emotion self. Welcome the emotion self into this day. When you are ready, breathe a breath of acceptance to the emotion self no matter what is found there. And only after this welcoming and this extending of acceptance do you notice if there is any emotion energy that is no longer needed that is ready to be released. And if there is, you just let it go. No force, no effort, just releasing. Perhaps you send it out with the support of the exhaled breath. Release it in whatever is your way. And if this has created any new spaciousness in your emotion self, you expand out the emotional health and wholeness that lives at your core into this newly opened space. You may also wish to partner this with breathing in the larger

emotion health and wholeness energy available from the larger universe outside of you. Breathe in and expand out to fill the emotion self with health and wholeness.

You can give this same gift now to your thinking mind. Taking time to pause and notice with loving awareness the thoughts and beliefs moving through the mind along with noticing any mental chatter present at this moment of this day. Pausing to notice the thoughts without the need to engage them and perhaps remembering that the thoughts are not necessarily your deeper truths.

After a few moments of noticing, you welcome your thinking mind into this day and this experience. Breathe a breath of acceptance to your mind. And only after noticing, welcoming and extending acceptance do you notice if there are any old beliefs that are no longer true for you or any mental chatter or thoughts that are no longer needed. If there are, and they are ready to be released, you just let them go. Perhaps with the support of your exhaled breath or whatever is your way. And if this creates any new spaciousness in your mind, you expand out the peace and wholeness that lives at your core to fill this space.

Again, you may wish to partner this with the peace and harmony that also lives in the world outside of you. Breathing in and expanding out peace and harmony for the mind.

Now you have created an environment where your wisest Self can emerge. And so you pause and breathe and be as this Self that is your true nature. You take all the time you need deepening your connection as this wise and expansive Self.

As this wise, expansive Self, you notice if there is any member of your inner human family that could benefit from exploring the land of sorrow. If there is, you know if this is the right timing for the exploration. If there is no need to explore the land of sorrow, its challenges and opportunities, or if the timing isn't right for the part that may benefit from this exploration, you merely allow yourself to rest in the environment you have just created with mind, emotion, body and spirit present.

If there is a part that can benefit from, and is willing to explore the land of sorrow, you find yourself sitting with this part in a safe and secure place. In preparation to explore this new land, you use this time to ready for the journey. Perhaps there are questions or fears that the exploratory part needs to voice. Perhaps this part needs to share with you its story of sorrow. Perhaps, this part needs reassurance that you are accompanying it on the journey into the land of sorrow. Perhaps this part needs to hear that if it enters the land of sorrow, it can also leave that land at any time. If there are ways of dressing, items needed for this travel, or anything else required, they are made available instantly. It is here that you are able to offer whatever is needed.

When the time is just right, this part of you that needs to explore sets out now into the land of sorrow. You are accompanied by your wise Self. You go as deep into the land of sorrow as is perfect for you at this time and, whatever memories are found here, whatever sights, sounds, and sensory experiences are evoked, you are offered the steady presence of your wise Self.

Any other guides or support that is needed is found along the way. If the emotion of sorrow rises up, you are offered unconditional love and witnessing. If re-experiencing of loss unfolds, you are not alone. If sharing is needed, you receive listening. Along the way you notice, without judgment, what this land is like for you.

What are the most dangerous places, or crisis places, for you? Of what are you most afraid? What do you need or how do you tend yourself in these places of the land of sorrow? Who is there with you? Are there any unexpected companions? Whatever unfolds, trust that it is just right for you. Perhaps you have been to this land before. If so, perhaps you notice the same or different ways of journeying. Perhaps this is your first visit. Just notice.

As you journey you also notice if there are any unexpected gifts or opportunities. There is no right or wrong in this. Just notice. You spend the perfect amount of time in this land of sorrow. And when it is time to leave, if you can, you gaze around and see if there is any gift, item or word that wishes to return with you as you exit.

You now begin to leave this land of sorrow. Your exit is accompanied by your wise Self and any other perfect companion or guides. Your journey out may be a different way or you may leave by retracing the path upon which you came. As you exit, just notice how you are. What are you seeing, sensing or feeling? What is the same or different for you after this journey into sorrow? Notice if you feel that this trip may, in some way, benefit the rest of your life.

You arrive back to the safe place where you and your wise Self began. Here you pause with your wise Self for the perfect amount of time to rest, share, integrate, question, claim, or whatever is just right for you. Perhaps you find yourself merging now with your wise Self in some way. Perhaps not. Whatever unfolds, you trust that it is just right for you.

And when you are ready you bring your awareness back to your breath. Breathing in, you notice breathing in. Breathing out, you *notice breathing out. You feel the surface of the place where you first began this meditation. You notice the temperature there. You return now, at your own pace, to ordinary awareness in this place. You open your eyes when you are ready. Gently you return knowing the journey was just the right experience for you. You may wish to journal about your experience.*

GOING DEEP

I awoke knowing that I must go deep. My father, coming from a family that has farmed for generations, would understand the need to leave nothing and harvest everything from this experience. I knew I must go to the depths emotionally and literally and the steep bluff trails at the Nebraska State Park I am visiting this Father's Day offer a tangible journey to the deep.

I make my commitment to go the whole distance, down to the bottom, to the river. I set my intention and ask for the blessing and companionship of Spirit. It isn't long when I realize the trail map (and I use that word lightly), is not going to get me there. Grossly inaccurate, missing many of the options for turns and changing directions, this map hands choice back to me. I trust my intuition and open to the possibility of making wrong turns or even starting over again.

And so through the deep wooded area and tall grass I go. What seems like the obvious, most direct route down the bluff turns out to be an overlook only about halfway down. It is beautiful here, this panoramic view of the Missouri River, its backwaters, the bluffs of South Dakota across the way. I stop and take it all in; the vastness, the perspective that I am small in this world, the building quiet, only the distant voices of any people now far behind me. I realize this stop is an unintended gift, but this dead-end path will not bring me to the bottom. So I retrace my steps over steep and sometimes tricky footing back to the place of choice. A quick request for guidance calls me to the left. This seems the least likely because of its flatness, yet I trust and go forward. The sun and shade take turns weaving through the trees. I go forward, still doubting my choice at times, and eventually there is a downward slope to the path, meandering left and right. It is a circuitous route, yet it *is* ever so slowly moving down. I am going deeper.

Suddenly, the slope pitches straight down more dramatically and I notice doubt again, this time about going too deep too fast. I keep going, remembering my commitment. Not long after I see stair-like steps in the earth going down. Whew! Good timing. Laughing, I go deeper still; it is mostly shade and darkness now, and I give gratitude for my walking stick.

Then suddenly, I see the bottom. Yes! I step out of the trees and darkness and into a flat, light, open and beautiful scene along the river and her backwaters. I am right next to the flow, no longer a bystander from a distance. It seemed like still water from so far away, but now I can touch and be present in her swift, gentle, ever-changing movement. Walking along the flat trail beside the river, I see a turtle sunning itself on a log.

Suddenly, she slips into the water and for a time swims beside me. We never know who our traveling companions will be, when they'll show up, or how far they'll go with us.

It's so ravishingly quiet down here. I've never seen nor heard one human being. After walking a distance alongside the river, I find a big stone bench right at the edge, a good resting place and refuge for contemplation, tears, reflection and gratitude. The turtle comes to visit three more times, swimming up river past me, down river and up river once again. Is it my imagination? She seems to be smiling at me. On the last pass, she travels with a tiny turtle companion of her own. As my time in the deep reaches a natural conclusion, I'm ready to return to the top. I give gratitude for the many gifts, companions and guidance.

Then I realize bringing this experience back up is its own challenge. It's probably good that I didn't think about this on the way down. I remind myself that I can pause as often as needed, and the darkness and shade are a comfort now. I pause often for water, wiping sweat from my brow. Slowly and steadily I climb the meandering path back. With a smile, I eventually pass the first trail I took and then, at last, arrive at the top, changed by the journey.

≈

Now I see that traveling the path of my Father's journey with cancer meant making a strong commitment to be present for all of it, the confusing places, the not-well-marked places, the choice points, the places with treacherous footing, even the deep, touching beautiful places. It meant trusting my inner soul map when no outer map could lead me. It meant appreciating what eased the way, like the water of compassion from the well of human kindness, like pausing to catch my breath. The walking staff of my partnership with Divine Presence that always adds safety to my footing, the reminders of this Presence during the journey's biggest choice points, and trusting the guidance received in spite of unlikely appearances and big doubts are some of the gifts brought fully up into the light. I have realized the challenges of the journey of going deep, yet I continue to harvest the surprising beauty, quiet and peace of that depth. It is in the silence that I can know more of myself and meet Divine Presence while remembering that I am not alone.

I am grateful for the journey.

Reflection Questions and Journal Prompts

- *What does this story evoke in you?*

- *Where are the places of going deep in your own life?*

- *Where are the places of journeying into the unknown where there are no maps? Who have been your companions on these journeys? What have been the challenges? What tools, coping or supports accompanied you?*

- *How do you care for yourself in the deep journey places of your life? Is silence part of this for you? Is being in the company of others part of this for you?*

- *Does the idea of commitment to going deep speak to you? Why or why not?*

- *Are there places in your life where you resisted going deep and, if so, why?*

- *Are there any places in your history where you have some yearning to go deep for some completion and integration around a particular chapter of your story? What or who might support you with that?*

Meditation on Going Deep

Begin by finding a place to relax where you won't be interrupted. Allow yourself to sink into this place of comfort and relaxation. Bring your awareness to your breath. For the next few moments, just notice yourself breathing. In and out. In and out. The breath fills and empties you. Breath by breath, you find yourself letting go of any tension, stress or mental chatter. Breath by breath, you sink into a place of relaxation. You feel yourself centered and peaceful, relaxed and at ease.

In this place of deep relaxation, you allow your consciousness to travel to a place of safety. This can be any place of your choosing: a beach, a meadow, a particular building or room. Trust yourself to know and arrive at the perfect, safe place for you.

In this safe place you become aware of all your senses. The sights, smells, sounds, and tastes are just right for you. Your skin and body feel just right here, too. Here in this place there is all that you need for your comfort and peace. You allow yourself to rest in this place.

Now you can choose to continue in this place and rest. You can also choose to leave this place and explore going deep. Whatever you choose, it is the perfect choice for you and is met with only love and acceptance of your decision.

If you choose to stay in this safe place and rest, you do just that. And if you are choosing to explore going deep, you make that inner commitment to travel with the perfect issue in your life, trusting that you will have safety and everything you need on the journey.

You ready yourself for the journey of going deep. You know all that you need to know about why you are called to the deep. You have all that you need for your body, your emotion self, your mind and your spirit on this exploration. You can travel alone in solitude or the perfect traveling companions are with you. It unfolds just right for you. Your journey may be symbolized by an outer journey as in the story. Or, it may be an inner journey or some of each. Trust and know that right now, it is unfolding just right for you.

The journey has begun. You are safe. You travel in the way and to the places that are most important for you. You are able to meet any challenges. You are able to express all that needs to be expressed and you have all the support you need for this. You marvel at your ability to go to the perfect depths around the issues that have called you. And while you may be called to move through sorrow or challenge, you know and trust your process is unfolding exactly as it needs to. You may be consciously aware of the meaning of your journey and you may trust that the meaning will be harvested over time. Every step of the way, you are guided. Take all the time you need now to journey in the way and time that is calling you. You follow your journey of going deep all the way to completion.

At the completion of your journey, you give gratitude for all that has transpired and to any helpers or companions along the way. You promise to take all the time you need to integrate within yourself this journey, in a way that is just right for you. And when you are ready, you return to the place where your journey first began. As you arrive there, you recognize that initial safe place. You may pause there for a time of rest before returning to ordinary consciousness.

Whether you have been resting in the safe place or journeying to the deep, when you are ready, you bring your awareness back to the place where you first began this meditation. You feel the structure supporting your body. You hear the sounds and notice any fragrances in your current surroundings. You notice the temperature and the presence of having skin that responds to this temperature. When you are ready, you take a couple of comfortable deep breaths and open your eyes. You take in your current surroundings. You allow yourself time to reorient here.

You may wish to journal about your experience or share it with a friend or companion.

STAYING SOFT

Her slight, frail body moved with increased lightness as we rounded the corner of the house to the backyard memorial garden. Our feet were guided by stepping stones with etched words of comfort . . . *Peace, Love Outlasts Everything, Beloved Grandson.*

We stepped around lush mounds of purple coneflowers, butterfly bush and shiny pots overflowing with purple and white petunias. We were caressed with birdsong, the warm, gentle breeze rustling the late summer leaves and lapping sounds as the lake moved in and out of the shore. Here and there garden prisms reflected the light that appears despite darkness.

Aunt Charlotte certainly knew about suffering, about physical pain and about loss. She moved through multiple hospitalizations with different cancers, surgeries and side effects from surgery. Physical pain could not keep her down. Each visit to the hospital or to her home while she was recovering left me marveling at her positive attitude, at her belief that God was watching over her, at her ability to undergo test after test and procedure after procedure without complaint. Though her resilience was unquestioned, the event that nearly swept her away was the sudden death of her beloved grandson, Danny, who died from a freak accident.

On this day, of what was to be our last visit, she needed to share Danny's garden. As we both wept, she told memory after memory of many rich times over the span of his short life. She told of how her last time of being with him was during a scheduled family gathering. She was so proud of how he, with wisdom beyond his years, sought out and connected deeply with each person present.

As we both wept I was struck again by her resilience and her faith, and the tangible display that even from tragedy beauty can be formed. I was moved by her ability to continue living with such an open heart.

In that garden I flashed upon a childhood memory of my own. I remembered how my sister and I would be gifted with visits to Aunt Charlotte and Uncle Darren's home on this nearby lake. I remembered how we kids would take their little rubber raft out on the lake. It was a small and shallow lake, and we would row out to the middle and get out of the raft. We would wiggle with our toes through the squishy mud at the bottom, searching to find the clams down there. We would grasp them with our feet, and then throw them in the bottom of the raft. After catching our limit of the day, we'd row back to the dock. There, we would lay the clams on the dock and wait for the sun to open them, not realizing that this involved the demise of the clam. Once the shells opened in the hot sun, we would search the meaty part of the clam for pearls. That's right—we were sure we would find valuable pearls. Of course we never did find pearls there. At least not the ones we were looking for.

Now, of course, I know that pearls come from oysters, that oysters' home is the ocean, not small and shallow lakes, that oysters open their shells and take in water. Sometimes a grain of sand will float in on this water.

As Rachel Naomi Remen M.D. says in her book, *My Grandfather's Blessing,* "Such grains of sand cause pain, but an oyster does not alter its soft nature because of this. It does not become hard and leathery in order not to feel. It continues to entrust itself to the ocean, to open and breathe in order to live. But it does respond." Remen continues with the following: "Slowly and patiently, the oyster wraps the grain of sand in thin translucent layers until, over time, it has created something of great value in the place where it was most vulnerable to its pain. A pearl might be thought of as an oyster's response to its suffering. Not every oyster can do this. Oysters that do are far more valuable to people than oysters that do not."

We all have pain and suffering. We have all experienced disappointment or hurt. Sometimes in this place of suffering or challenge we might harden. Sometimes we can stay soft and vulnerable and find gifts in that suffering. And like the oyster, sometimes, this vulnerability over time creates a gift of extraordinary value.

I shared my newly surfaced memory with my aunt along with my reflections about her ability to stay soft in spite of life's challenges. It seemed that our garden tour, and the life it engendered, offered up the pearls I had been waiting for. I can't wait to string them together.

Reflection Questions and Journal Prompts

- *What speaks to you in this story?*

- *What are your childhood memories of joy and exploration?*

- *In your stories of pain, disappointment or suffering, where have you found yourself hardening against the pain and suffering? How did this affect your life and relationships?*

- *Where have you found yourself being able to stay soft and open during the pain and suffering? How did this affect your life and relationships?*

- *What are the pearls for you, places of increased value, in your life that resulted from being open and moving through pain, perhaps in a shared way with another? Maybe you will find a way to string your pearls together.*

Meditation on Staying Soft Through Pain

Begin by finding a place to relax where you won't be disturbed. Find a place there to sit or lie down. Allow yourself to take a couple of comfortably deep breaths. Let your exhaled breath assist in emptying your body of any tension that is ready to be released. Let your exhaled breath assist you in emptying your emotion self of any tension that is ready to be released. And let your exhaled breath assist you in emptying your mind of any mental chatter that is ready to be released. Breath by breath, you find yourself relaxing into your center. Breath by breath, you are more at home in yourself.

You may stay in this place and continue to breathe and relax for the duration of the meditation. If this is the choice for you, know that it is met with complete acceptance and you stay right here relaxing now.

Or, you might choose instead to take a journey of staying soft and not hardening during pain or suffering. If this is the choice for you, make an inner commitment to the journey and an inner agreement to begin. As this journey begins, you find yourself traveling down a path toward a safe and special place. Perhaps you journey alone or perhaps there is a guide, helper or companion with you. You travel along this path until you reach the perfect place to experience staying soft through pain. You allow yourself to sit or lie down here, in solitude or with your helper. In this place your breath deepens and you know that you have everything you need to support you in this experience.

When you are ready, you first anchor your body in what you know to be its experience of centeredness. This might mean a sense of muscle relaxation, a steady heartbeat, a certain way of breathing deeply, or some other sensations. You also anchor your emotion self in a way that speaks to its centeredness in being able to experience all emotion beyond the place where we've learned to label the emotion as "good" or "bad." This might include the ability to stay soft and open in the heart and belly. Additionally, you anchor your mind in its place of centeredness. This may mean being able to observe thoughts without engaging them. This may mean being able to remember that the thoughts aren't necessarily your deeper truths. In essence, you are anchoring yourself in your Authentic, Wise Self, your Expansive Self, and your large Spirit Self.

Take time now just to breathe and become very familiar with what it is like to be in this Expansive Self. Notice how it is for your body, emotion self and mind. Allow yourself plenty of time to deepen your relationship with this part of yourself. Breathing in and out, anchor here in your center. Breathing in and out, deepen your connection with this true you.

Now when you are ready, you allow a place of deep pain, suffering or loss to come into your awareness. As you allow this to surface, without holding back you just notice how it is for your body. Are there any changes from the body's place of centeredness? No judgment here. Just notice. As you allow this pain to surface you also notice how this is for your emotion self. Are there any changes from the emotion self's place of centeredness? And as you allow this suffering to surface, you also notice how this is for your mind. Are there any changes from mind's place of centeredness? Remember there is no judgment. Just notice. Just notice if this surfacing of pain, loss or suffering takes you somewhere out of the centeredness that you are at your core.

See if you can both honor the suffering the way it is in the body, and allow it to move through like a wave and then return to the body's place of center. See if you can both honor your suffering the way it is in the emotion self, allow it also to move through like a wave and then return to the emotion self's place of center, of soft heart and belly. See if you can both honor the suffering the way it is in the mind, allow it to move through like a wave and then return to the mind's place of centeredness and peace. Practice staying soft and open, yet unattached, to the sensation and experience of the suffering. If you find yourself hardening, avoiding or just mentally processing the suffering, just invite yourself to return to the place of allowing the experience of the suffering, on all the levels that you are, so that you can return, again and yet again, to the place of center. This place of center both honors and allows the experiences and sensations, and yet does not resist the suffering nor does it cling to the suffering. This can be hard work and yet you know that this is the place of your wisdom. This is the place of both/and. This is the place of forming pearls of extraordinary value.

When you are ready, you begin to retrace your steps back to the start of this path that you have taken. It is here that you take all the time you need to integrate your experience. It is here that you give gratitude for whatever you have learned. It is here that you give

147

gratitude for the whole of your experience without judgment. It is here that you say thank you to any helpers. It is here that perhaps you receive a symbol, object or word to help you remember your ability to be in your center, to be soft and open to all experiences of your life.

When you are ready, whether you have been relaxing or journeying, you begin to bring your awareness back to the place where you first began this meditation. You notice the surface that has been supporting your body. You notice the air, sounds, and smells of your environment. You allow yourself a couple of comfortably deep breaths and when you are ready you open your eyes. You give yourself all the time you need to reorient to your surroundings.

You may wish to journal about your experience or share it with a friend or companion.

THOSE WHO HAVE COME BEFORE US

The path I walk, the journey I travel has often been made clear by others who have gone before me. My previous breast cancer experience made this teaching perfectly known.

During the diagnosis and treatment of that breast cancer, my heart was more open than ever. For me, this meant, in part, tears, copious tears. Oh sure, I cried when I was afraid and sad, less often when angry about the inconveniences mostly, and most often, most generously, I cried when I felt love.

I felt love right from the beginning as compassionate professionals spoke with me about the process I was entering. I felt love in the presence of my amazing surgeon who understood that there would be a Larger Presence in the operating room (and we weren't talking about the anesthesiologist).

I felt love from my radiology oncologist who finally verbalized after many tears shed in his presence, "You know, Cindy you're going to be better off in the end because of how you honor your feelings."

"You bet, Doc!" was more kind than saying, "Yes, I told you so!"

I felt love in the touch of my tattoo artist as she prepared my body with the marks for radiation. As a side note, my nephew, sporting "full sleeve" tattoos is not impressed with my version of tattoo! I felt love from my radiology techs, especially the one who told me her mom was a breast cancer survivor and that she saw the same kind of courage in me. I felt love from my intuitive, amazing acupuncturist who helped me relax and open to healing through my series of radiation treatments. I felt the presence of deep love living right alongside fear in the waiting areas of my oncologists. I felt immense love from my partner, friends, and family who expressed this in a myriad of ways.

I found my experience to be an invitation to more heart openness, more realness, no masks, no pretending, no false pride and ego. This invitation came during times of great fear and imagining the worst. It also came during times of vast gratitude and love. I released self-protection in a way that opened me to more vulnerability that could be seen as the gift of authenticity.

Ironically, because of this vast compassion, love and gratitude, there were times during this life saving treatment experience that I remember thinking, *If I die right-here-and-now, it would be a happy death.*

I believe that a kind of bliss waits for us on the other side and I believe that we do not have to wait until then to welcome it. We can have it now, too, if we are really present to the totality of our experience. I believe that to embrace the deepest love and bliss stuff, we also have to allow ourselves to embrace the deepest dark stuff too. They come together. This is the paradox of life and someone once said that to be able to hold the paradox is a sign of spiritual and emotional maturity. I have not been perfect at this by any stretch of the imagination. But, the breast cancer journey has given me an opportunity to practice this.

A phone call six months after my radiation treatments introduces me to Anita, a divorced young mother of two children. She asks to schedule an appointment saying, "I will explain what I need when we meet." During that first session in my office, it becomes clear that Anita does not know of my former cancer experience and yet, surprisingly, she begins this story. Two years prior to our session she was diagnosed with breast cancer. Her cancer was the exact same kind as mine. Her treatments and surgery were also the same and occurred at some of the same places though she had different health care practitioners. She did *not* have the same loving experience that I had. She had not felt held in love and respect.

Anita described herself as a forgiving person and she was frustrated and baffled by her intense and lingering anger. In spite of the variety of ways she had tried to move beyond resentment about how she was treated, she felt stuck in her suffering. In the middle of sleep she would awaken and find herself replaying places of disrespect and misunderstanding. She felt overly sensitive and irritable and believed that her relationships were suffering. She told me her close friends were terrific and yet, no matter how compassionate they were she didn't think they could understand her experience. She just couldn't let it go and she was asking for guidance, ideas, support.

Not only did Anita not know about my breast cancer, it turns out that she also did not know that part of my work is guiding people through a particular model of forgiveness. Had she come to see me before my cancer experience I believe I would have held her story quite well and been able to support her. But, because of my cancer experience, I could offer her empathy in a deeper way. I shared with her enough of my story so she could know I understood something of her journey. I told her of the specific kind of forgiveness work that I love and invited her to think about entering that process.

We were both blown away by the synchronicity of all this. When I asked her how she decided to come and see me, she said, "I heard your name, not from someone else but, from somewhere in the ethers. That's a new experience for me and I don't really understand it." Clearly something mysterious was unfolding. With tremendous courage, Anita did enter the forgiveness work and, upon completion, felt free.

What is also significant here is that at the end of Anita's difficult treatment she gave honest feedback. She pushed for change in places she believed would have made her experience more humane. I believe that because of this, Anita helped all of us who came after her have a better experience. She was one who had gone before to lead the way.

Another of those "leaders" who have come before us is my friend, Jessica. At the time of her breast cancer surgery, in the mid to late 1990s, she agreed to an experimental procedure. This procedure, the removal of the sentinel lymph nodes, just the one or two nodes nearest the breast with cancer, has made a remarkable difference for many women. Prior to this new diagnostic tool, the surgeon would remove a whole section of lymph nodes to test for cancer, resulting in life-long problems with lymph drainage for that woman. Now the sentinel lymph node removal is standard procedure and has spared many women the extreme swelling and often-severe complications of more lymph node removal.

The recognition of the importance of those who come before us is not limited to a journey of cancer. It can be found and honored in many places. My pioneer ancestors cleared the land for my generation of farmers. Early social workers cleared the way for those currently practicing social work. The path I walk and the experiences I have, are often made easier, kinder and more loving, by those who have come before. Bless those who have been willing to go before.

As we journey, may we also remember that we, too, are clearing the path in our own unique way for those who are yet to come.

Reflection Questions and Journal Prompts

- *What, if anything, speaks to you from this story?*

- *Where are the places in your life where you have been gifted by those who have come before?*

- *Where are the places in your life where you may have cleared the way for others?*

- *In those places, what has been your own unique way of journeying?*

- *Do you have stories, like Anita, of being drawn mysteriously to the right place or person at the right time? If so, what are those stories?*

- *In the above story, the experience of holding the paradox of bliss and suffering is mentioned. Are there similar stories in your life?*

- *What are the stories in your own life that have offered a gift of vulnerability?*

- *Where are the places of challenge that have moved you to more authenticity?*

- *In what ways would you like to have your life offer a kinder, easier and more loving path for others?*

Suggested Activities or Experiences

- *Perhaps you are called to draw, paint, sculpt or dance your own holding of the paradox, two seemingly opposite things.*

- *Maybe you wish to take a walk, do a dance or engage in some other art medium that is about releasing self-protection, persona masks, or ego. Maybe you take a risk and share your more authentic self with someone.*

- *Maybe you wish to take one day, one week, or one year living in gratitude for those who have come before you. If you do, just notice what this is like for you.*

- *Maybe you wish to take one day, one week or one year living consciously as if to clear the way for others. If you do, just notice what this is like for you.*

Meditation With Those Who Have Come Before

Begin by finding a comfortable place to sit or lie down where you won't be disturbed. Close your eyes if that is comfortable for you. Allow your awareness to come to your breath. For now, just notice the breath. In and out, in and out. Let the breath breathe you. Be breathed by the breath. Take all the time you need right now to just be with the breath.

And when you are ready, you welcome your body into this day, into this experience. Begin by bringing loving awareness to the body. Just notice how the body is at this moment of the day. There is no need to change anything and there is no judgment, only loving awareness of the body.

Notice any places of tension, discomfort or holding. Notice any places of ease, flow and comfort in the body. Welcome the body into this experience, this day and breathe a breath of acceptance to the body. Only after extending awareness, welcome and acceptance to the body do you notice if there is any tension, holding or energy in the body, that is no longer needed, that is ready to be released. If so, then you just let it go, perhaps sailing it out on the exhaled breath. And if this created any new spaciousness in the body you can use your breath to expand out the health and wholeness that lives at your core into this newly opened space.

You may also wish to partner that with breathing in the wholeness energy available in the larger universe outside of you. Breathing in, and expanding out health and wholeness for the body.

You can extend this same welcome to the emotion self. Begin by noticing with loving awareness whatever emotions are present with you this moment of this day. No judgment, no right or wrong, no need to change anything. For now just notice the emotion self. Welcome the emotion self into this day.

When you are ready, breathe a breath of acceptance to the emotion self no matter what is found there. And only after this welcoming and this extending of acceptance do you notice if there is any emotion energy that is no longer needed that is ready to be released. And if there is, you just let it go. Don't force. Don't effort. Just release. Perhaps you send it out with the support of the exhaled breath. Release it in whatever is your way. And if this has created any

154

new spaciousness in your emotion self, you expand out the emotional health and wholeness that lives at your core into this newly opened space.

You may also wish to partner this with breathing in the larger emotion health and wholeness energy available from the larger universe outside of you. Breathe in and expand out to fill the emotion self with health and wholeness.

You can give this same gift now to your thinking mind. Take time to pause and notice with loving awareness the thoughts and beliefs moving through the mind along with noticing any mental chatter present at this moment of this day. Pause to notice the thoughts without the need to engage them and perhaps remember that the thoughts are not necessarily your deeper truths.

After a few moments of noticing you welcome your thinking mind into this day and this experience. Breathe a breath of acceptance to your mind. And only after noticing, welcoming and extending acceptance do you notice if there are any old beliefs that are no longer true for you or any mental chatter or thoughts that are no longer needed. If there are, and they are ready to be released, you just let them go.

Perhaps with the support of your exhaled breath or whatever is your way. And if this creates any new spaciousness in your mind, you expand out the peace and wholeness that lives at your core to fill this space. Again, you may wish to partner this with the peace and harmony that also lives in the world outside of you. Breathing in and expanding out peace and harmony for the mind.

Now you have created an environment where your wisest Self can emerge. And so you pause and breathe and be as this Self that is your true nature. You take all the time you need deepening your connection as this wise and expansive Self.

When you are ready, you allow your imagination to take you to a safe place in nature. As you arrive in this safe place, you notice how pleasing it is to all your senses. The sounds are comforting and nourishing. The fragrances expand the depth of your breath. You find every muscle relaxing in the temperature that is just perfect for you. All that your eyes behold brings a deep sigh of gratitude.

You may remain in this place relaxing or you may now choose to journey with those who have come before.

If you are choosing to journey, you now notice the appearance of several other beings whose presence seem to open your heart. You realize that they have come here to be with you. They invite you to walk with them on a lush and beautiful path.

You feel a sense of deep love and compassion radiating from them as you all journey together. You notice your sense of calm. After a short distance there is a fork in the path. Your guides and companions take you first to the path that veers to the right. As you proceed, it becomes clear that along this path, you are reviewing some experiences from your life. In this review you are able to see, sense and know how your life has been enhanced by others who have led the way.

You may even have a sense of these others in a specific way. Perhaps they are recognizable and known by you or perhaps they are not. But as these places in your life are revealed to you in new ways, you feel a deep sense of gratitude. You express this gratitude, in ways just right for you, to those who have come before to clear the way. You may even be given some guidance about future experiences that have yet to unfold. Perhaps you give gratitude for those who are going before you in the future.

When you feel completion on this branch of the path you and your companions return to the place of the fork. At this time you are encouraged to lead the way down this part of the path that veers to the left. Your companions and witnesses follow closely behind.

As you proceed, you find a new appreciation for how you have led the way, cleared the path for those who have come after you. This unfolds in specific or general ways that are just right for you. You find you have a deeper sense of compassion and love for yourself and the ways your life path has held meaning for others known and unknown to you. You give gratitude for this new awareness, this new view of your life.

When you feel completion on this branch of the path, you, your companions and witnesses return the way you came. You reach the fork in the path and continue all the way back to where the path began, arriving back to the safe place in nature where you first began.

Here you find your own way to thank your traveling companions and receive any gift or blessing they offer as a way of anchoring your experience. Honoring your own pace and timing you pause to give gratitude and integrate this recent unfolding.

When you are ready you allow your awareness to return to the place where you first began this meditation. Breathe and acclimate back to this place before entering the next part of your day.

You may wish to journal about your experience or share it with a trusted friend or companion.

THE SOIL OF MY ANCESTORS

The question of how to celebrate my 50th birthday had been rumbling around inside me for several months. Since traveling brings such enjoyment for me, I thought a trip would be a perfect way to cross that half-century threshold. Hawaii had been on the travel wish list for some time and since that felt like a big trip and turning fifty felt like a big trip, too, I began to explore the options. I even purchased the book *Hawaii for Dummies*.

Weeks went by. My partner and I took in much information, explored many ideas and pondered many possibilities. Nothing seemed clear; nothing was falling into place. Finally, I acknowledged that Hawaii didn't seem like the way to honor this celebration. I was able to say aloud that it felt like no matter how much information we crammed in, no matter how wonderful Hawaii was, no matter how many stories of the islands we heard, trying to make Hawaii work was just that—work.

I sensed there was something different, something more, waiting to make itself known. Then, just days after we decided against Hawaii, an informational brochure about a tour to France, England and Scotland showed up in the mailbox. I got goose bumps. This was it! This was the trip; this was the 50th celebratory trip!

I have always felt a kinship with France. I knew that my father's ancestry began in France and I had minored in French in college, not that I remembered much of what I learned. I had spent a weekend in Paris with a friend while visiting her family in Germany many, many years before and had felt a deep yearning to return and explore my paternal roots one day. And now, that day was coming.

My partner and I sent in our registration, as did my cousin—the family genealogist. We all began counting down the days until our departure while immersing ourselves in the tour information.

The tour schedule allowed only one free day and it fell during our time in Paris. We decided that was the day the three of us would take a train, rent a car and find our way to Channay-Sur-Lathan, the farming village of my ancestors. In the 1600s, Pierre Chicoine left that village and traveled to Montreal, Canada, where he settled. The Chicoine family branched out from there over the next 400 years. Now, nine generations later we were returning to the ancestral soil.

My cousin and I both come from farm families in southeastern South Dakota. Before we left, we visited our family farms and took samples of soil from our respective farms then baked it to destroy any microbes that might contaminate French soil. So packed amidst my toiletries, clean clothes and maps rested this little vial of South Dakota soil. I have always felt a strong connection to the farmland that my grandfather, father, and, now, my brother farm. My heart still opens and expands when I visit there, and this strong connection only deepened after my dad's death. I missed him and felt his presence journeying with me in that vial of soil.

The thirteen days of the regular tour were really, truly wonderful, and we saw much, experienced the kindness of many people and wore ourselves out taking it all in. But the highlight of it all was that day in the French countryside. That free day began with us rising early and finding our way to the train station, buying our tickets and climbing on board.

In Paris, we were fortunate to be among people who spoke English very well. Since our French was quite limited, especially mine, this eased our way in navigating foreign transportation. When our train arrived in the city of Tours, the luxury of everyone speaking English faded fast as we tried to get our rental car. Eventually we got the car and directions we thought we understood, and headed to the much smaller country roads.

The countryside was so beautiful. Birch or aspen tree groves, fields of blooming canola flowers, and fresh May breezes seemed to be guiding our way. Gradually, we found our way to the tiny farm village of Channay-Sur-Lathan. We parked our car and began to walk around the streets of the village. The houses were quaint and shuttered in French country style. We walked past one older, slightly worn house that had a courtyard beyond the old ornate fence with gardens that were so lush they looked almost wild. "Look, there's the Secret Garden," I joked.

We kept going and found the old Catholic Church, now a historic landmark only open on certain days. The church was locked but we peered through the keyhole to see the old pews and the altar with sunlight shining magically through the stained glass windows. We took our photos by the post office and at the very edge of town we found the cemetery. There were many, many Chicoine headstones there. I felt as if I was connected by invisible strands through the ages to my tribe.

The cemetery was held on its perimeters by farm fields. We went to the edge of a cornfield. New, tiny corn plants rose from fertile sandy soil. We didn't know if this was a Chicoine field, but this place was offering itself for a ritual. I knelt down in the earth and took out the soil vial from my pocket.

As my tears began to flow, the sky clouded over and it began to rain. I cried warm tears of sadness and grief, tears of deep love for my dad and for the soil he so loved, and for the ancestors who had come before us and the soil they tended. I opened my vial and shook some rich black South Dakota soil into my hand. I asked for it to be blessed, I gave thanks for the long lineage of farmers, tenders of the soil that reside still in my bones and spirit. My fingers spread open and the grains of South Dakota soil sifted onto the French soil. In gratitude, I gathered a bit of soil from this field far away from my home, and yet *of* my home, and placed it in the second vial I'd brought. As soon as my tears dried and I stood, the clouds cleared and the sun came out. It was as if the sky were weeping with me. A healing had taken place in a way that was unanticipated, supported by a Presence beyond my own imaginings.

This wasn't the only surprise. Later, we wandered around the village and showed several people our drivers' licenses with our Chicoine name on them. Many smiled and gasped delight at the name and pronounced our name aloud, exactly as we had grown up hearing it. Only now it seemed musical. We settled for those gasps and lyrical speaking of our last name because none of us could communicate in French very well. We did find a man in a bakery who pointed down a street then pointed at our name on the license. We thought he meant that we still had kin living here. So, we followed what we understood from his pointing and our limited understanding of French directions and came upon the "Secret Garden" home. How fun was that? We went to the door and knocked. The door opened and an older woman and her adult son looked at our drivers' licenses, saw our name—their name—and invited us in. They spoke no English, we spoke the tiniest of French, and yet we spoke beyond the words from the depth of our hearts, celebrating the miracle of our connection. They showed us a family photo on the bureau, pointed to someone and said, "Canada." The smiles and hugs were more important than the attempts to communicate with words. We were home in each other's hearts. Reluctantly, we left to catch our train and finish our structured tour.

Shortly after I returned home, I visited my family farm in South Dakota. I asked my brother if I could go to one of the cornfields for a ritual. He was all for it. I found the cornfield and knelt among the tiny corn plants coming up through rich, dark earth. I reached in my pocket and shook into my hand some of the now-sterilized sandy soil from Channay-Sur-Lathan. I asked for it to be blessed. I gave thanks for the long lineage of farmers, for those who plant, tend, harvest, and then rest the soil. I gave thanks for the way they have blessed my life, how they live in my bones and spirit. I sprinkled the French soil onto the South Dakota land and stirred it together.

I keep a tiny bit of this mingled soil in my home. It reminds me of my heritage. It reminds me of the courage of journeying outside our homeland, of not being too attached to where we think we need to go and to be open for the something different, something more that is waiting to make itself known. It reminds me of following our dreams, of pausing to feel our connections to things beyond our understanding. It reminds me of how we are held by those no longer on the earth and yet still of the earth. It reminds me of how deep in my bones, I belong to a people I don't need to know personally. It reminds me of how deep in my bones, I belong to the earth.

Reflection Questions and Journal Prompts

- *What, if anything, do you connect with in this story?*

- *What are your stories of not forcing things, of being open to what calls you, open to something different?*

- *Can you relate to having a sense of belonging or connection to a time, place or people that you don't know personally? How do you explain things beyond logical understanding?*

- *What are your stories, or your ancestors' stories of journeying outside the homeland and following our dreams? This might be a literal sense of journeying or a symbolic one.*

- *What are your stories of connection with your ancestors, with place, with the earth?*

Suggested Activities or Experiences

- *Angeles Arrien, a cultural anthropologist and author, speaks of the ancestors as those who have gone before us into the greatest of the unknowns—death. Because of this, she says we can ask them to help us in our lives as we face any great-unknown places, including our own death. You might explore your ancestral connections, if you haven't already. You might also consciously speak to them for that guidance in any places of doubt or mystery in your life right now.*

- *If it appeals to you, you might design your own ritual of connecting with your ancestors.*

- *You might spend a day imagining that you are walking with the friendly ancestors of your lineage. Notice what this is like for you.*

- *You might imagine walking through a day as the ancestor who is offering guidance with one of your descendants. Notice what this is like for you.*

- *If you imagine your descendants exploring your life years from now, what would you want them to know about you? You might write, sculpt, paint, draw or express something in any other art medium that would tell them about you.*

- *Do you have a descendant, or other relative, in your life right now that you would like to visit or with whom you would like to offer some stories or wisdom? Maybe you will seek them out. If you do, just notice if you have certain expectations. If so, try letting them go and being open to whatever flows.*

Meditation on Meeting Your Ancestors

Begin by finding a comfortable place to sit or lie down where you won't be disturbed. Allow your awareness to come to your breath. For now, just notice the breath. In and out, in and out. Let the breath breathe you. Be breathed by the breath. Take all the time you need right now to just be with the breath.

And when you are ready, you welcome your body into this day, into this experience. Begin by bringing loving awareness to the body. Just notice the body and how it is at this moment of this day. There is no need to change anything and there is no judgment, only loving awareness of the body.

Notice any places of tension, discomfort or holding.

Notice any places of ease, flow and comfort in the body.

Welcome the body into this experience, this day and breathe a breath of acceptance to the body. Only after extending awareness, welcome and acceptance to the body do you notice if there is any tension, holding or energy in the body, that is no longer needed, that is ready to be released. If so, then you just let it go, perhaps sailing it out on the exhaled breath. And if this created any new spaciousness in the body you can use your breath to expand out the health and wholeness that lives at your core into this newly opened space.

You may also wish to partner that with breathing in the wholeness energy available in the larger universe outside of you. Breathing in, and expanding out health and wholeness for the body.

You can extend this same welcome to the emotion self. Begin by noticing with loving awareness whatever emotions are present with you this moment of this day. No judgment, no right or wrong, no need to change anything. For now just notice the emotion self. Welcome the emotion self into this day.

When you are ready, breathe a breath of acceptance to the emotion self no matter what is found there. And only after this welcoming and this extending of acceptance do you notice if there is any emotion energy that is no longer needed that is ready to be released. And if there is you just let it go. No force, no effort, just releasing. Perhaps you send it out with the support of the exhaled breath. Release it in whatever is your way. And if this has created any new spaciousness in your emotion self you expand out the emotional health and wholeness that lives at your core into this newly opened space.

You may also wish to partner this with breathing in the larger emotion health and wholeness energy available from the larger universe outside of you. Breathe in and expand out to fill the emotion self with health and wholeness.

You can give this same gift now to your thinking mind. Taking time to pause and notice with loving awareness the thoughts and beliefs moving through the mind along with noticing any mental chatter present at this moment of this day. Pausing to notice the thoughts without the need to engage them and perhaps remembering that the thoughts are not necessarily your deeper truths.

After a few moments of noticing you welcome your thinking mind into this day and this experience. Breathe a breath of acceptance to your mind. And only after noticing, welcoming and extending acceptance do you notice if there are any old beliefs that are no longer true for you or any mental chatter or thoughts that are no longer needed. If there are, and they are ready to be released, you just let them go.

Perhaps with the support of your exhaled breath or whatever is your way. And if this creates any new spaciousness in your mind, you expand out the peace and wholeness that lives at your core to fill this space. Again, you may wish to partner this with the peace and harmony that also lives in the world outside of you. Breathing in and expanding out peace and harmony for the mind.

Now you have created an environment where your wisest Self can emerge. And so you pause and breathe and be as this Self that is your true nature. You take all the time you need deepening your connection as this wise and expansive Self.

Now you can choose to remain in this place of breathing with and as your Self or you can prepare to take a journey to meet your safe ancestors, relative or relatives. If you are choosing the ancestral journey, when you are ready, you find yourself exploring a path in a place that is safe for you, in a way that is safe for you. In this journey you have all that you need to feel secure in the journeying. You move along the path until you see an open area or clearing up ahead. As you near the clearing you see or sense that there are others there waiting for you. As you come even closer you realize that these others are your ancestors or relatives, the one or ones who are safe for you to connect with at this time in your life.

Perhaps those waiting there are ancestors that you have met in your life. Perhaps they are ancestors you have only heard stories about.

Perhaps these ancestors are introducing themselves to you for the first time.

Perhaps there are generations of ancestors gathered there. You trust whatever it is that unfolds.

You enter the clearing in your own way and at your own pace. You notice how you are welcomed. You notice whatever degree of kinship you feel with these beings.

Perhaps you find yourself speaking and listening.

Perhaps you find yourself communicating in ways beyond words.

Perhaps you share stories of challenge or celebration.

Perhaps you have questions to ask and perhaps their wisdom is shared with you.

Perhaps things are shared that give you new understanding of your own life.

Perhaps what is shared offers comfort for a particular challenge.

Perhaps what is shared gives you good council on how to proceed in a particular area of your life.

Perhaps there is a ritual of connectedness that you participate in together. You engage in whatever experience is just right for you.

As you near the end of your time together, perhaps these ancestors help you record a message of your own for your future descendants when, and if, they come exploring to this place.

As you prepare to say goodbye for this time, knowing that you can return any time to be together, you give gratitude for all that has transpired.

Perhaps they send you with a word or symbol that will help you to remember this experience. You retrace your steps back to the place where you began on the path.

When you are ready, whether you have stayed breathing and relaxing or journeying to your ancestors, you begin to bring your awareness back to the place where you first began this meditation. You notice your breathing and feel your body resting on the surface where your meditation started. You take a couple of comfortably deep breaths and open your eyes taking in the sights and sounds of the place you began. You give yourself all the time you need to re-orient to your surroundings.

You may wish to journal about your experience or share with a trusted friend or companion.

PART THREE:

Turning Around the Heart of Transformation

We open to transformation. We can transform on personal levels by the transformation of our fears, limitations, challenges and differences. We can transform through surrender, being hollowed out, forgiveness and prayer. Transformation can be a kind of lighthearted reverence or a more serious reverence and it can come in expected or surprising ways. Often after we have experience with our personal transformation, we notice ourselves living, breathing and being the presence of transformation for the larger world, for the larger universal and cosmic transformation.

THEMES OF LETTING GO

We are anticipating a great night's sleep after a rigorous travel day to our camping spot on St. John's in the U.S. Virgin Islands. The bay breezes and surf sounds are lulling us into a sleepy stupor. At dark, we walk past the picnic table on which sits our cooler with the strongest of latches, and we enter our tent on its raised platform. Hours later we awaken from a deep sleep to a persistent rustling sound. After we remember where we are, we grab a flashlight with trembling hands, turn it on and shine it outside the tent where the rustling has only gotten louder. A large dark shape comes into focus. For crying out loud, it's a donkey. It has found a way to unlatch that major clasp on the cooler and is undeterred by the flashlight, or by our shaky voices yelling, "Get away from there." All we can do is watch as it rustles around in the cooler and chomps on our just purchased delicacies for several lunches and dinners. Welcome to the island culture! After several minutes, we are relieved when the donkey finally wanders away. Wondering if it is safe, we chance going outside to check out the damage. We shine the flashlight in the cooler and discover our fine foods are still perfectly sealed and all appears well. So what was the donkey eating? Then it hits us—the only thing missing is our garbage sack, the one that held banana peels, apple cores and wrappers from a couple of energy bars, and perhaps other things we don't remember. This is weird, just plain weird. It is as if our donkey came in, sifted and sorted, then took only our garbage. Suddenly, we begin to laugh. We laugh until we cry. We laugh from exhaustion, from relief, and from the absolute weirdness of this.

The next morning, we talk about the previous night's marauder and we can hardly believe what happened. We both have the sense that maybe we dreamed it or maybe just made it up. But together we corroborate the event.

"Wouldn't it be grand," I said, "If we all had an 'inner donkey' to sort and sift and take out our inner trash, leaving all the good stuff behind?"

This seems like a great way of letting go of what we no longer need. "Inner Donkey"–I can imagine it now!

≈

Each morning, I sit at my altar. The top of the small chest in my front window is a sacred space in my home. The touchstones on it help me remember who I am, help me remember that there is something larger than my small self. These things also remind me that something larger inside me connects me to the Everywhere Presence all around me. The items change from time to time, but their reminders remain the same. You might see my prayer beads, my inspirational reading, my feathers and stones, prisms, singing gongs or bowls, or my statues. You would also notice a plaque that says, "Bless All the Paths our Feet Walk to be Free." Each day, before I enter the world, I sit before these touchstones and remember, pray, meditate, listen. It is the only way for me to anchor in the larger sense of who I am, what I call the High Self.

If I don't take time to sit here, then I inevitably forget the bigger picture, forget to keep my heart open, forget to be open to the blessings and miracles of this day before me. If I don't sit here, I lead with my ego self, who focuses on right and wrong ways of doing things, who can be critical and judgmental, who sees only successes and failures, and who weighs things on a much different scale than my Higher Self. My days tend to be more about struggle and fear, hurrying and getting things done and less about process and flow and gifts in everything when I do not make time to sit here. Sitting here is essential for me to live a conscious life.

One morning, however, I have a busy mind. Many thoughts are moving through. I have a zillion to-do lists and my mind is racing over which one to tackle first. I am also revisiting, analyzing, and ruminating over yesterday things. This is exhausting and I try to skip beyond all that to the peacefulness that lives at the core of who I am. This is easier said than done. I feel like getting up and just getting to some of the many things calling for my attention. But I know better. I keep my butt planted in that chair and breathe, just breathe. It's a Monday and it's garbage day. I hear the familiar roar of the garbage truck at our neighbor's house.

Great, just great, I think. *Just more noise in an already noisy world.*

170

The truck pulls up to the curb in front of our house. The automated gizmo comes out from the side of the truck where it grabs the partner gizmo on our garbage bin and lifts. It hoists the garbage can up, tips it upside down and empties out all the trash. Then it drops the bin right back on the ground. I start to laugh. That garbage bin is like my mind this morning, full of trash and junk and stuff ready to be released. Wouldn't it be grand if my own Higher Self Recycling Truck could just stop by every day, maybe several times a day if needed, and empty me? Just turn me upside down and shake out all the trash, the old beliefs and thoughts that no longer serve, the past issues that need to be let go of, future things that I can ruminate on to the point of distraction, and anything else that just takes me to a place of forgetting, of losing my perspective. This appeals to me. I think I will surrender today to the Higher Self Recycling Truck.

≈

A few years ago, I was returning from lunch in a van filled with colleagues. All of us were enjoying the beautiful fall day. The sky is a beautiful blue and the leaves are showing their vibrant orange colors. We pull up to a stop sign in a residential neighborhood and as we wait for the light to turn green, we hear a loud droning sound and all turn in its direction. None of us can believe our eyes: A man, with a very large leaf blower, is blowing the leaves out of the tree. I am not kidding. He was blowing the leaves out of the tree. I exploded in laughter, and we all laughed at the ridiculousness of hurrying that fall process.

Wait a minute, I then thought; *let's not be too quick to judge. How many times do I try to hurry something that needs to take its own time? How many times do I try to force something that just needs to flow its own way?*

There is a time to let go, and sometimes we hang on too long. And sometimes we try to move things too quickly. Right timing isn't always so easy to discern. Okay, a guy blowing leaves out of the tree–funny? Yes, but humbling, too.

≈

I was in an annual speech contest in high school. We could choose debate, or focus on a humorous or inspirational reading. Sometimes I chose humor, but most often I chose a dramatic inspirational reading, something that touched the heart. One year, I wanted to enter the inspirational category again, but I couldn't find a speech that really spoke to me from the teacher's selection. I asked if I could pick something on my own, with her approval, for the contest. She agreed, but stressed that she must first screen it and approve. No problem.

I had a drawer full of inspirational things at home, and I went there and dug through it. At the bottom was an old copy of the book *Bambi* by Felix Salten. One chapter still held a weathered bookmark. I took it out, sat on the floor and read.

It was autumn and there were two leaves talking to each other about how so many of their friends had gone, fallen off the branches and never returned. Leaf by leaf, they fell, leaving only those two last leaves. Those left behind were sad and questioning the meaning of life. They spoke of loss and memories. At times, they annoyed one another and other times, they gave each other great comfort. Eventually, they both let go into the great mystery. That was the piece I chose, I suppose because in some way the themes of loss, meaning, and letting go were working in my own life then. My teacher approved of this choice and so, as I practiced being with these great lessons through a classic story, I felt the words, the story, healing me, teaching me. I did well with that piece at the contest, and I still remember the judges' silence, the unexpected pause and smiles after I finished. It is a holy moment I remember.

$$\approx$$

Letting go is a big topic. There is the letting go of the busyness of the mind. There is the letting go of old beliefs and ways of thinking. There is the letting go of things that don't really matter, like whether or not the next barf stain from our beloved aging cat will come out of the carpet.

There are larger places of letting go—the loss of jobs, status, the need to be right, facing illness, the ending of relationships, the launching of children from the nest, the fading of a youthful body, the death of loved ones and our own mortality. I am counting on my Inner Leaf Blower, my Inner Recycle Truck, and my Inner Donkey, maybe even lessons from classic literature, for help when it is my time to say goodbye.

EEE-haw!

Reflection Questions and Journal Prompts

- *What, if anything, about these stories speaks to you?*

- *What are your own stories of letting go?*

- *How do you discern when you are letting go too soon or when you are hanging on too long?*

- *What supports you in letting go when it is time? What supports you in hanging in there, not rushing the process, if that is what you are called to?*

- *When you find yourself letting go, do you take time to consciously welcome into that newly opened space what you wish to live there?*

- *Are you able to thank what you are letting go of for what it has given you, for how it has shaped you or helped you?*

- *Do you have a sacred space in your home for centering? If so, what things have you gathered there that play a part in your remembering who you are. Are these things always the same or do they change over time?*

Suggested Activities or Experiences

- *If you don't have a special place in your home to center, pray or meditate, perhaps you might create that for yourself.*

- *If you do have a centering place, perhaps you will look at this place with fresh eyes and confirm that everything there is relevant for you now. Perhaps some changes could enhance your centering time. If so, perhaps you will make those changes.*

- *You might write a poem, create a drawing, painting, or sculpture about letting go.*

- *You might play a piece of special music and do a dance or movement about letting go. Maybe, in this dance, you are the donkey, the garbage truck, the leaves on the tree in Bambi, the leaf blower releasing too soon, or something else entirely. Trust yourself to know.*

- *Perhaps you walk with the intention of guidance about the balance of letting go and continuing to hold. Perhaps you intend this for a day, a week, a month or longer. Once again, trust yourself to know.*

- *Once you have a letting go experience, perhaps you welcome into that newly opened space all that you wish to reside there.*

Meditation on Letting Go

Begin by finding a comfortable place to sit or lie down where you won't be disturbed. Close your eyes if that is comfortable for you. Allow your awareness to come to your breath. For now, just notice your breath. In and out, in and out. Let the breath breathe you. Be breathed by the breath. Take all the time you need right now to just be with the breath.

When you are ready, welcome your body into this day, into this experience. Begin by bringing loving awareness to the body. Just notice the body and how it is at this moment of this day. There is no need to change anything and there is no judgment, only loving awareness of the body.

Notice any places of tension, discomfort or holding.

Notice any places of ease, flow and comfort in the body. Welcome the body into this experience, this day and breathe a breath of acceptance to the body. Only after extending awareness, welcome and acceptance to the body, notice if there is any tension, holding or energy in the body that is no longer needed, that is ready to be released. If so, then you just let it go, perhaps sailing it out on the exhaled breath.

If this created any new spaciousness in the body, you can use your breath to expand out the health and wholeness that lives at your core into this newly opened space. You may also wish to partner that with breathing in the wholeness energy available in the larger universe outside of you. Breathing in, and expanding out health and wholeness for the body.

You can extend this same welcome to the emotion self. Begin by noticing with loving awareness whatever emotions are present with you this moment of this day. No judgment, no right or wrong, no need to change anything. For now, just notice the emotion self. Welcome the emotion self into this day. When you are ready, breathe a breath of acceptance to the emotion self no matter what is found there. And only after this welcoming and this extending of acceptance do you notice if there is any emotion energy that is no longer needed that is ready to be released. And if there is, you just let it go. No forcing, no effort, just releasing. Perhaps you send it out with the support of the exhaled breath. Release it in whatever is your way.

If this has created any new spaciousness in your emotion self, you expand out the emotional health and wholeness that lives at your core into this newly opened space. You may also wish to partner this with breathing in the larger emotion health and wholeness energy available from the larger universe outside of you. Breathe in and expand out to fill the emotion self with health and wholeness.

You can give this same gift now to your thinking mind. Take time to pause and notice with loving awareness the thoughts and beliefs moving through the mind along with any mental chatter present at this moment of this day.

Pause to notice the thoughts without the need to engage them and perhaps remember that the thoughts are not necessarily your deeper truths. After a few moments of noticing, welcome your thinking mind into this day and this experience. Breathe a breath of acceptance to your mind.

Only after noticing, welcoming and extending acceptance do you notice if there are any old beliefs that are no longer true for you or any mental chatter or thoughts that are no longer needed. If there are, and they are ready to be released, just let them go with the support of your exhaled breath or whatever is your way. If this creates any new spaciousness in your mind, expand out the peace and wholeness that live at your core to fill this space. Again, you may wish to partner this with the peace and harmony that also live in the world outside of you. Breathe in and expand out peace and harmony for the mind.

Now you have created an environment where your wisest Self can emerge. And so you pause and breathe and be as this Self that is your true nature. You take all the time you need to deepen your connection as this wise and expansive Self.

Perhaps the meditation up to this point is all that you need for re-connecting with the body/mind/emotion and spirit's wisdom of letting go. If so, allow yourself to stay in this place of connection with your expansive Self for as long as feels right for you and then return to ordinary consciousness and the environment where you first began this time.

If you would like to go a bit deeper with the theme of letting go, then allow your imagination to take you on a journey. Make that inner commitment and agreement to journey.

In your imagination, find yourself transported to a special safe and sacred space. In this place, notice all that surrounds you. This place is pleasing to all your senses. What you see is perfect for you. What you smell, taste and hear is perfect for you. Whatever sensations are present for your body is perfect for you, too. You are delighted to be in this place, feel very safe here and find that you are willing to keep exploring.

From the distance, you see a helper or guide approaching. Perhaps this guide is your expansive Self. Perhaps it is a new or familiar helper. Whoever it is, it is the perfect helper for your journey to the place of letting go.

Your helper approaches you and you feel only unconditional love and acceptance. When you are ready, you and your guide start out along a path that takes you to the sacred place of letting go. Along the path you notice your awareness is heightened and that you accept whatever sensations, emotions or thoughts arise about approaching the place of letting go.

Soon you are there. This is the place of letting go. There is everything you need here for a ritual of letting go.

First, your guide and you sit and find clarity about whatever needs to be released. You are able to discern, with help if necessary, what is ripe for releasing. If there is any additional preparation for your ceremony of release, you enter into it. And when you are ready, you now enter into your ceremony of release. You have all the time you need. You have all the support you need. You trust the unfolding of all this to support your letting go.

Once your ritual is complete, you take all the time you need to integrate your experience before you return on the path to the place your journey began. When you are ready, you give gratitude for all that has taken place, thank your helper and return on the path to your beginning place. As you return, you notice how you feel the same or different from when you began. There is no right or wrong, you merely hold a sense of loving awareness. As you arrive at the place where you began, you trust that you have all that you need to continue any integration of your experience and the filling of any newly opened space with all that you wish to reside there; all that is meant to fill you.

When your journey of letting go feels complete for this time, knowing that you can return at any future time, you once again give thanks and prepare to return to ordinary consciousness. There may be a gift, a word or symbol given to you to take back with you to remember this time of letting go.

Now you begin to reorient to the environment where you first began this meditation. You feel the structure of the surface that has been supporting your body. You notice the temperature in that environment. You take a couple of deep breaths and, when you are ready, you open your eyes. Take all time you need before moving on to the next part of your day.

You may wish to journal about your experience, share it with a friend or companion or enter into additional ceremonies of letting go for yourself. Trust yourself to know.

FACE THE FEAR

Ear-piercing screams radiated like the lightening through the dark night. Eddie, who was always very afraid of these Midwestern storms, had been awakened by the rumbling thunder. Mom was awake now, too, and sprinted to her 4-year-old son's room. He looked so tiny sitting straight up, eyes wide with terror, in a bed that dwarfed him. She went to him, sat on his bed and brought him close to her. Feeling his body tremble with powerful sobs nearly broke her heart. She felt powerless to reassure him at times like this.

After Eddie had calmed some, she heard herself say, "What do you think we should do?"

More fierce thunder and crackling lightening punctuated the long pause. The whole room lit up once again. Eddie eased his body ever so slightly away from her firm hug. In the mere inches that separated them, he raised his head and in the glow of the next lightening flash she could see a new sense of determination in his eyes. "We should play the *Face the Fear* game."

"OK" she responded, thinking, "I wonder what that is." Rallying she added, "What do we need to play?"

With a voice no longer quivering, Eddie said, "A cape."

With his hand firmly in hers, they went to the bathroom and grabbed the first "cape" they could find. She tied the bright-striped terry cloth cape around his neck. "Now what?" she asked.

"We have to go outside to the driveway."

The storm's sounds were farther in the distance and so without hesitation they went out the front door to the driveway. Eddie released her hand and began to run, up and down the driveway gathering momentum and yelling at the top of his lungs, as only a super hero can, "Face the Fear! Face the Fear! Face the Fear!"

Quickly, Eddie's mom joined in, and they ran together, screaming into the quieting night until they were coughing and sputtering from uncontrollable laughter.

Not only did Eddie face the fear, he felt it, too, *and* made it all the way through to the other side. As his mom tells the story, they referred to this experience often in the coming years and even still into Eddie's adulthood. When sadness or worry entered their lives, one or the other would say, "What do you think we should do?"

"Face the Fear. Face the Fear," the other would say.

≈

Jimmy had been beside himself with excitement ever since his mom had told him they were going to a major amusement park for vacation. This park had it all, water rides, gigantic rollercoasters, and thrill rides too numerous to count. Finally, the eventful day arrived and they were ready to embark on their first excursion, *The Cave of Surprises*. Tickets were purchased and Jimmy and his mother waited in the long line. When it was their turn, they entered the damp, dark enclosure. They were guided as if blindfolded to a seat in one of many linked cars. They could hear the mumbled voices, but could see no one. Chug, chug, chug, the ride began as they lurched forward. Picking up momentum, they began a trip of steep inclines and rapid descents as they were jerked around tight corners and curves. Torrents of splashing water, frightening objects bursting forth out of the cave's darkness, and a number of other surprises had Jimmy snuggling closer and closer to his mom. She could feel his tiny body shaking and sense the panic building in him. Loud screams and vigorous laughter emanated from the other riders but not a sound came from Jimmy. When the ride was finally over, Jimmy wouldn't talk about it and would only say that he wanted to go back to the motel. His mom felt sick inside and berated herself for not anticipating this situation. Swimming and a video arcade kept them busy at the motel, but Jimmy had clearly lost his zest for this trip. That night, Mom read him a story, kissed him good night and hoped that Jimmy wouldn't have nightmares about the ride.

The next morning over their continental breakfast, Jimmy's mom asked him what he wanted to do.

"I want to go back to the ride," he said.

At first, his mom thought she hadn't heard him correctly and so she asked again, "What do you want to do today, Jimmy?"

"I want to go back to the ride."

"Are you sure?"

"I'm sure, Mom."

Jimmy resisted any further discussion. Though she questioned the wisdom of this plan, she honored Jimmy's request and once again they traveled to the amusement park, purchased tickets and stood in line with an even larger group of people.

Jimmy and his mom overheard the little boy in front of them pleading with his parents. "I'm scared. I don't want to do this. Don't make me go," he said.

The boy's older siblings teased him about his reluctance. After a few minutes, Jimmy lightly tapped the boy on his shoulder. The boy turned to face Jimmy.

Standing tall, Jimmy spoke, "Yesterday, I thought this was scary."

The other little boy looked at him for a moment, nodded and moved silently with his family in the line toward the ride.

Jimmy had never heard of Eddie's *Face the Fear* game, but he played it with class and style.

≈

Sharon, a beloved nurse in a small town, traveled to the outpatient-counseling clinic where I worked. What Sharon didn't tell me until she successfully ended therapy, was that coming in for counseling was her last option. On her own, she had tried many ways to stop the pain from newly recovered memories of childhood abuse. But these memories were taking over her life and she couldn't sleep, couldn't eat, and couldn't relate to her loved ones. She was having trouble keeping the effects of this from interfering with her work, and that was something she couldn't and wouldn't tolerate because of her deep commitment to her patients. She told me that if therapy didn't work she had a partially loaded gun at home and had planned to end her life.

Thankfully, Sharon never got to that point. We began our work focused on initial coping and ways to contain the memories as we gently explored their impact on her. Many things improved as time passed, but one lingering issue loomed large—Sharon had a repeating nightmare.

In the nightmare, Sharon finds herself in a dark, dark hallway with many doors on each side. Suddenly, she feels a presence behind her. She hears a wild growling sound. Hot breath makes contact with her neck, and the hair on her arms stands up. As she begins running away, she risks a brief peek behind her. Chasing Sharon is a huge, drooling, fangs-bared, ferocious lion. She knows that if he catches her, she will be torn apart.

With legs that feel leaden, Sharon tries to run for her life. She wildly zigzags from door to door in a panic. They are all locked. None of them will grant her safety. She tries to scream but nothing comes out. Gasping for breath, heart pounding, tears streaming down her face, unable to scream, this is the place she awakens.

Courageously and with dedication, Sharon examined the dream and its symbolism. She willingly explored ways she would creatively change the nightmare to a reasonable conclusion, if she had the power to do so.

Then came the session when Sharon walked in with a smile of satisfaction on her face. She sat down and told me of her dream from the night before. She is still in the dark hallway with many doors. The ferocious lion is still chasing her. She still feels his hot breath and hears his growling. She knows his sharp teeth are still bared, ready to tear her to shreds. She is still running. Only this time, Sharon stops, turns around, and faces her lion.

Immediately, the lion pauses in surprise. Drooling, he roars at her. Their eyes meet and he sees that Sharon isn't backing down.

Then it happened. A miracle. The lion's gaze shifts from threatening to curious, he quiets, his teeth no longer visible, his whole countenance softens. Unbelievably, Sharon finds herself reaching out her arms. He rises up on hind legs and they embrace. He disappears. Sharon tries the doors. They are all open to her. She can go anywhere she chooses.

Tears in both our eyes, Sharon unrolls a huge collage. She has a large spiral of images pasted on the poster board. She tells me the story of the images. It begins in the upper left hand corner. Images of destructive fire are arranged together. There is a gun tucked in among them. As the spiral moves on the images change. There are dozens of question marks and faces of obviously suffering girls and women. There are clocks surrounded by impatient faces. Then small images of faces no longer contorted in pain. Gradually, faces with small smiles appear. Nature scenes of peace where families are happy together round another bend in the spiral. The word peace is found at the end with the spiral trailing off into the unknown.

Sharon's nightmare never reoccurred.

In the Christmas cards she sends to my office each year, she tells me that she is doing well and is fully engaged in life. She is happy and at peace. She tells me I made such a difference, and I respond by telling her *she* is the one making the difference. I still share the collaged-poster she gave to me with other clients as a way to offer hope. Instead of the Russian roulette she had planned, Sharon played *Face the Fear* and made it through.

Thunderstorms, amusement park rides, reoccurring traumatic nightmares, and any number of other things. We all feel afraid sometimes. How we are with fear makes all the difference. So meet me in the driveway of life. We can admire each other's capes.

Reflection Questions and Journal Prompts

- *What stirred up fear for you when you were little? How did those around you react? How did you react? What messages did you grow up with about fear? Are you aware of any childhood fears that still influence your life?*

- *What do you fear now? Do your ways of being with or thinking about fear today resemble your childhood ways? As an adult, do you share your fear with others? How do they react?*

- *Are you satisfied with your ways of being with fear now? If not, who and what might be able to support you in new strategies for feeling the fear, facing the fear and finding yourself on the other side of each wave of fear?*

- *If you collaged your own story of fear what images would appear? If it feels right to you, make a collage as Sharon did.*

- *What are the places, things and people who remind you of hope when you are afraid?*

- *If you carried a symbol of hope in your pocket what would it be? You are invited to carry that symbol.*

- *Are you aware of inspiring others to face their fears by having faced your own?*

- *How might your facing of a fear lead to inspiring others?*

Meditation on Transforming Fear

Begin by finding a place to relax where you won't be disturbed. Close your eyes if that is comfortable for you. Begin by noticing your breathing. Allow the breath to support you in softening and opening your being in this exploration. Allow yourself to find a safe place in which to explore a fear in a way that can transform it or allow you to move through the fear.

In your safe place, let your senses explore. What sounds, sights, smells and sensation greet you there? Just notice. Make any adjustments that make this place even safer for you.

Off in the distance, you notice a wise guide and helper. He or she is coming toward you radiating love, compassion and strength. As your guide approaches, you notice eyes of loving wisdom beaming at you. This wise helper offers to guide you through a current fear. You may choose to go with your guide and transform a fear or you may choose to stay in this place and just relax. The choice is yours and this guide offers you unconditional love regardless of your choice.

If you choose to say no to the exploration of a fear, you may choose to remain in this safe place with your guide and relax and take time just for being.

If you choose to go with your guide, he or she will help you pause until you are able to discern what fear you wish to walk with. Your guide will also prepare you with whatever skills, tools, objects or supplies that will be needed along the way. Once you are ready, you and your guide set out along the path of fear transformation.

Perhaps you walk with your fear to a place where it is released in a ritual. Perhaps you walk through the valley of fear with your guide at your side until you move completely through the fear. Perhaps your guide teaches you the magic of fear transformation. Trust that the perfect experience unfolds for you as you and your guide work in partnership. Allow yourself to pause now and experience your own process.

When you are ready, allow yourself the time and space to claim your courage, your strength, your new wisdom. Perhaps a ritual of claiming this experience unfolds now or later. Perhaps an object or symbol comes with you to remember the possibility of fear transformation that you can carry into the future. Take whatever time you need to feel complete in this journey.

Only when you are ready do you thank your guide for whatever has transpired. And only then do you begin to allow your consciousness to return to the place where this meditation began. You reacquaint yourself with your breath, the temperature on your skin, and the sounds in your locale. When you are ready you open your eyes. You allow yourself space and time to integrate your experience.

When you are ready, you may wish to share your experience with another or your journal.

BUILDING OUR NESTS

On our deck the brightly colored strips of cloth blowing in the breeze at first seem to be eye candy. But if you look more closely, you can see words written on the cloth, "For peace on our planet," "Madie's health is restored," "I pass my exam in the fall," "That no one goes hungry." These are prayer flags, an adaptation of an ancient Tibetan tradition.

And in Nepal and Tibet, you may well see squares of colored cloth floating in the breeze. They hang in the barren, mountainous countryside, in the middle of what seems like nowhere. They also hang near homes, temples and bridges. They hang everywhere. These people believe that as the wind blows, the prayers are carried out into the universe and the prayers themselves bless all that they touch in that wind journey. These global prayers then become a blessing to all beings as the wind carries them. When the writing is no longer visible it is believed that the prayers have been answered.

Several years ago at a retreat, we were invited to write our prayers on strips of bright cloth of varying patterns. We then reverently tied our modified prayer flags on a rope that covered a great distance as it hung between the trees. To see so many prayers, written by so many people blowing in all directions brought tears to many eyes. It was as if we could feel the energy of the prayer being lifted up and out by the wind and carried off to the place where it could be heard and answered. We paused in awe, our gaze shimmering through eyes of light.

A couple of years after that prayer flag experience, I was involved in a two-year program with some incredible women. I offered the prayer flag experience to them and they scooped it up. Each quarter that we met, the women added prayers to the strand. I would bring fabric cut into strips: plain cloth of reds, pinks, yellows and blues, patterns of starry nights, green spring ferns, autumn paisleys, many choices for many prayers. The women would write their heartfelt prayers. There were very personal prayers for the health of self and loved ones. There were prayers for hope during suffering. There were political prayers, spiritual prayers to keep the faith, and an incredible number of prayers for our planet and for all beings across the globe. Many believe that when we pray for one, we pray for all and that a prayer of health for someone in particular is actually a prayer of health for all. It certainly felt as though these prayers were large enough for all. It was humbling to be present with them.

The plan was that I would keep all the strands from our retreats and we would join them together for our final gathering. In between gatherings, I would hang the growing strand on our deck and offer it to the breezes of winter, spring, summer and fall.

Come fall, I noticed something peculiar. I noticed there were a couple of places where all that remained of a prayer flag was a small nubbin of cloth hugging the rope. I thought maybe the cloth was eroding, that it just fell away and the prayers were complete. But I noticed day after day that another nubbin and then another. Soon, the nubbins were growing rapidly in their numbers. I wondered what in the world was going on, and set up camp to watch from the window to see if I could catch a glimpse of what was unfolding. One day, the mystery was solved—the squirrel looked first here and there, then when it seemed the coast was clear, it brazenly leaped on the rope and began to tug and pull, pull and tug until it had a prayer flag. It then scrambled up into the big maple tree with the cloth hanging from its mouth. I meant to get to the bottom of this. Was it a game, entertainment for the squirrel realm? I had to find out.

So I expanded, moved my camp outdoors one day, waited and watched. I positioned myself under the big maple tree, where rustling sounds grew louder, and soon I could see bits of dried leaves falling to the ground nearby. Then I saw him. First, tentative and cautious, then boldly, he moved branch by branch to the deck and planned his landing right there by the prayer flags.

Kurplunk!

Yanking and pulling, gnawing and chewing. As soon as the squirrel got his new flag, he jumped, branch by branch, higher and higher, into the tree where he disappeared into the yellowing foliage. I figured he was gathering the flags to shore up his nest for the coming winter. For the first time ever, I found myself yearning for the trees to shed all their leaves even though I am not a fan of winter. But I wanted to move things along so I could see if the prayer flags were visible in the squirrel's nests.

Nature, as she always does, moved at her own pace. Weeks later, having half-forgotten the squirrel's antics, I arrived home from the office. A bit of green caught my eye as I moved from garage to house, so I looked up. A large, make that *very* large, squirrel's nest was perched high up in the maple tree. This nest was woven with several different pieces of colored cloth, green and pink, blue and yellow, patterns of this and that, and interspersed with dry leaves forming the most amazing— and largest—nest I have ever seen. It was a work of art. A *large* work of art! The piece of green, which had originally caught my eye, was woven into the nest on one end and the other end flew freely in the cool autumn breeze. It was as if the squirrel had written his own prayer upon the cloth now joined in unison with prayer flags everywhere.

I watched that squirrel and his nest all winter. It gave me great joy to think of him sleeping, all curled up, warm and cozy, held in a weaving of prayer while his own prayer was carried out into the universe.

Prayer comes in many forms and we never know how and when and by whom our prayers will be answered. I have learned that nests come in many forms too. I am learning to watch for the unexpected, to be a witness to the mystery, to weave my nest with prayer.

Reflection Questions and Journal Prompts

- *What are your beliefs about prayer? Where do these beliefs come from?*

- *What are your experiences with prayer?*

- *If you participate in prayer, what does that sound like for you? What does it look like? What is your process of praying?*

- *If you pray, are there certain places in which prayer feels more comfortable for you? Is there a special place in your home where you pray? Are there certain places in your community that lend themselves more easily for your prayer?*

- *If you were to write prayer flags today, what would be your prayers for yourself? What would be your prayers for others? What would be your global and universal prayers?*

Suggested Activities or Experiences

- *If prayer is compatible with your belief system, you might make your own prayer flags and hang them somewhere in your environment.*

- *You might make a prayer box and place your prayers on slips of paper into the box.*

- *You might write a poem about prayer or that is a prayer.*

- *You might play a special piece of music and move as a prayer, a body prayer.*

- *You might dedicate one entire day to moving in the world as a prayer for others. You might dedicate one entire day to moving in the world as a prayer for yourself. You might just move in the world each day with your life as a prayer.*

Meditation on Resting in Prayer

Begin by finding a comfortable place to sit or lie down where you won't be disturbed. Close your eyes if that is comfortable for you. Allow your awareness to come to your breath. For now, just notice the breath. In and out, in and out. Let the breath breathe you. Be breathed by the breath. Take all the time you need right now to just be with the breath.

When you are ready, you welcome your body into this day, into this experience.

Begin by bringing loving awareness to the body. Just notice the body and how it is at this moment of this day. There is no need to change anything and there is no judgment, only loving awareness of the body.

Notice any places of tension, discomfort or holding.

Notice any places of ease, flow and comfort. Welcome the body into this experience, this day, and breathe a breath of acceptance to the body. Only after extending awareness, welcome and acceptance to the body, do you notice if there is any tension, holding or energy in the body, that is no longer needed, that is ready to be released. If so, then you just let it go, perhaps sailing it out on the exhaled breath. If this created any new spaciousness in the body you can use your breath to expand out the health and wholeness that lives at your core into this newly opened space. You may also wish to partner that with breathing in the wholeness energy available in the larger universe outside of you. Breathing in, and expanding out health and wholeness for the body.

You can extend this same welcome to the emotion self. Begin by noticing with loving awareness whatever emotions are present with you this moment of this day. No judgment, no right or wrong, no need to change anything. For now, just notice the emotion self.

Welcome the emotion self into this day. When you are ready, breathe a breath of acceptance to the emotion self, no matter what is found there. And only after this welcoming and this extending of acceptance, do you notice if there is any emotion energy that is no longer needed and is ready to be released. If there is, you just let it go. No force, no effort, just release.

Perhaps you send it out with the support of the exhaled breath. Release it in whatever is your way. And if this has created any new spaciousness in your emotion self, expand out the emotional health and wholeness that lives at your core into this newly opened space.

You may also wish to partner this with breathing in the larger emotion health and wholeness energy available from the larger universe outside of you. Breathe in and expand out to fill the emotion self with health and wholeness.

You can give this same gift now to your thinking mind. Take time to pause and notice with loving awareness the thoughts and beliefs moving through your mind, along with any mental chatter present at this moment of this day. Pause to notice the thoughts without the need to engage them and perhaps remember that the thoughts are not necessarily your deeper truths.

After a few moments of noticing, you welcome your thinking mind into this day and this experience. Breathe a breath of acceptance to your mind. And only after noticing, welcoming and extending acceptance, do you notice if there are any old beliefs that are no longer true for you or any mental chatter, or thoughts that are no longer needed. If there are, and they are ready to be released, just let them go.

Perhaps you can do this with the support of your exhaled breath or whatever is your way. And if this creates any new spaciousness in your mind, you expand out the peace and wholeness that lives at your core to fill this space. Again, you may wish to partner this with the peace and harmony that also lives in the world outside of you. Breathing in and expanding out peace and harmony for the mind.

Now you have created an environment where your wisest Self can emerge. And so you pause and breathe and be as this Self that is your true nature. You take all the time you need to deepen your connection as this wise and expansive Self.

You can remain here breathing and resting, or you can choose now to take a journey of building your own nest. Whatever you choose, it is met with unconditional acceptance. If you choose to stay here, you do just that.

If you choose the journey, you make an inner commitment and agree to explore. You begin to set out on a journey to collect all the prayers that are needed and wanted to build your resting place or safe nest. You find yourself in a safe place where all that you need to build your nest is readily available.

It may be that you journey on a path where various prayer flags are hanging all around you and you select the perfect ones for your nest.

It may be that you find yourself in a fully supplied artist's studio and you make all the prayers you need to form a perfect resting place or nest for yourself.

It may be that you are called to make a safe-place-nest that you will return to again and again.

It may be that you are called to make a safe-place-nest just for this day or moment. Trust yourself to know. Allow your inner wisdom to take the journey and find whatever supplies are needed to unfold the perfect experience for you.

When you have all the prayer flags you desire and any other materials, you begin to assemble your nest, your safe resting place. If you need additional supplies, you discover that they are magically available to you. You take all the time you need until you have formed the perfect safe-place-nest for you. When the time is right, you crawl, fly or in some way, enter your nest. Perhaps you spend just a few moments in your nest today. Perhaps you spend a longer time there. Trust yourself to know.

Now, notice how your nest is. How does it feel to be surrounded by the perfect weaving of prayers just for you? How does it feel to be snuggled in a place of prayer? You spend the perfect amount of time just being in this prayer.

Whether you have been resting in the initial resting place of this meditation or in your prayer nest, you begin now to return to your ordinary consciousness. You prepare to return to where this meditation first began, knowing that you can return to this time and place any time you desire.

Notice the structure that is supporting your body. Notice the temperature in the place where you first began welcoming and extending acceptance to your body, emotion self and mind. Take a couple of comfortable deep breaths. And when you are ready, open your eyes. You allow yourself the perfect amount of time to reorient yourself to your waking consciousness.

You may wish to share your experience with a companion or journal about it.

FORGIVENESS

The antiseptic scent permeates everything. My dad and I stand at Uncle Warren's bedside. He has brought us here to his deathbed. His physical presence is releasing itself from this world, and I have come to say goodbye. His breathing is raspy, and I am unsure if he can really hear me. I trust that his spirit knows I am there. I wish him a safe and easy voyage to the Great Mystery. Tears stream down my face as I share this last earthly connection with him. My dad reaches in his pocket, takes out his white cotton handkerchief and wipes away my tears.

It was such a simple gesture—my dad wiping away my tears—but it took decades for us to get to that point. I was born a crier. I cry when I'm sad, happy, and angry and when my heart is opened by love. If I don't tear up at least once a day, I think something must be wrong and my heart must be closed.

But I didn't come to this place naturally; I grew up in a generational farm family. We didn't cry. We were stoic. We kept our business to ourselves. I have come to value my tenderness and sensitivity, but when I was growing up, it was definitely seen as weakness.

Take, for example, the Christmas when I was seven or eight years old. I had wanted a particular doll for what seemed like a long time, and opening the package that held the doll was so potent to me that I cried. Moments later, I was still teary when my siblings and I were lined up by the fireplace for our yearly Christmas photo. My dad, trying hard to get a good photo I'm sure, yelled at me for crying. But as a crier, of course, I then cried more, out of embarrassment and maybe shame. In the photo, I am red-eyed and red-faced. It wasn't a happy moment.

Then and now, I loved my dad more than words could ever express—and yet, I resented his judgment about my crying and expression of emotion. It created a little barrier between us. Oh, we carried on over the years creating new and wonderful memories of all kinds. We laughed, joked and loved in powerful ways. My relationship with him was strong and deep, yet there was this place of separation from him in ways that I didn't like or want. The resentment I felt toward him about this took energy needed for other things in my life. So I tried rationalizing it away by understanding how my dad grew up and where he came from. I offered it up to the God of my childhood. I prayed for forgiveness. And yet there it was, always niggling at me.

As a therapist, I worked with many different models of forgiveness. I knew the value of forgiveness. I spoke with my clients about forgiveness. And yet, forgiving my dad for his disdain of my tears was something I couldn't just use my mind and my religion to release. I, of course, blamed and criticized myself for this. I remember thinking, "Something is wrong with you. How can you possibly help others if you can't live a resentment-free life?"

And then I encountered a forgiveness model formed by Edith Stauffer, PhD, called "Unconditional Love and Forgiveness." In it, forgiveness is about choosing to stop suffering because of other's shortcomings and it doesn't mean that what happened is okay. In this model, our human self, the part of us that suffers, is given space to release the suffering in a way that we can then reconnect with our transpersonal self, the part of us that can love unconditionally and can find peace even after the most horrendous wrongs or tragedy. In this work we use an empty chair for the person, who doesn't need to know we are doing this. We do this work for us. It isn't about changing the other person or the other person needing to change in order for us to forgive. This work also offers a way for us to forgive ourselves.

This way of finding forgiveness was—is—a great fit for me. I use it all the time for myself and with others. And I used it to forgive my dad around the issue of my crying and emotional expression.

It is clear to me that forgiveness changes our inner world. What is remarkable and mysterious is that something in the larger universe also changes, and if we are lucky, we get a glimpse of how that outer world has shifted. I completed the process of forgiving my dad just a couple of weeks before we found ourselves with Uncle Warren as he was dying. I believe Dad's wiping of my tears, after all those years of a very different pattern around my tears, was a glimpse at the mystery of this outer-world change.

I believe when we do our forgiveness work it opens a doorway that the person we are forgiving can walk through or not. This is a doorway of the possibility of change for them. This doorway presents itself even when the person doesn't consciously know that forgiveness has taken place. That was true I think for my dad who gradually shifted his way of being with emotion. One of my clients says this best, I think. She does forgiveness work on her own, often. But, occasionally she will call and say, "This is a really big one. Will you guide me through a forgiveness session with _____? I am ready to stop sending "F-You" vibes out into the universe."

When we stop sending "F-You" vibes out into the universe, I think that opens up new possibility for change. You couldn't scientifically prove it, I suppose, but that's what I think.

Here are some other remarkable glimpses of how releasing resentment can offer potent changes in our lives and in the lives of others:

≈

❖ Tallia is an adult survivor of childhood sexual abuse perpetrated by her grandfather. She kept this a secret from most of her family of origin for many years. At some point, her cousin found out and told her story to everyone in the family. While he may have been trying to advocate for her, she felt that this was her story to tell. She was furious with him and the resulting resentment created an emotional and physical cut-off from her cousin. Even though this extended family was close, if there were family gatherings where her cousin would be, Tallia refused to go. She also refused to invite him to any of the major events in her own life, or the lives of her children. There was no communication, no phone calls, no e-mails, and no contact whatsoever. Tallia even had trouble uttering his name. The anger was big and it ate away at her. Eventually, Tallia knew she needed to let go of her suffering about her cousin's actions. She successfully moved through the forgiveness process. Her cousin knew nothing about her doing this. After years of absolutely no contact, about two weeks after she let go of her resentment, he called her. He asked for forgiveness and apologized. Something in the universe had shifted. Ever so slowly they began to rebuild their relationship.

❖ Martha, a woman in her sixties, came in for forgiveness work. She was in a lot of emotional pain from an abortion that she'd had as a teenager. She was simultaneously stressed by increasing respiratory problems and on a great deal of medication for asthma and other possible health concerns. After completing the groundwork for forgiveness, Martha released her self-resentment about the abortion. At the end of that session, she looked at me intently, and with surprise. "You're probably going to think I'm crazy," she said, "but I don't think

I'm going to need my inhaler anymore. I'm breathing the best I have in years right now. But will this feeling last?"

Martha still calls me periodically to report that she is doing remarkably well. She is on minimal medication, is steeped in gratitude for the freedom she feels and has been guided to do volunteer work with a local adoption agency.

❖ Geraldine's grandmother died many years ago. Geraldine felt her niece's actions during their grandmother's dying process were neglectful and abusive. From that time on, their relationship had been severed. But her resentment toward her niece wasn't Geraldine's only reason for seeking therapy—she was also suffering from numerous health issues, including severe ulcerative colitis.

She was barely surviving on the minimal nourishment she took in. Pain and cramping was a daily occurrence. Geraldine agreed to do forgiveness work as a piece of her healing. During the catharsis step, she found herself screaming at the empty chair that represented her niece, "You make me sick. You make me sick." At the end of her session, she said, "Somehow I feel like my colon is healed. I don't think I am going to need all my crazy medications anymore. I think I can actually eat normally and I am hungry for the first time in months." After talking to her physician, he reluctantly reduced her medications. She has felt only minor digestive upset and has felt healthier than ever.

≈

There are many definitions, ways and methods of forgiveness. What is most important is that through forgiveness magical things can, and do, happen. I believe that forgiveness is necessary for our mental, emotional, physical and spiritual health. I believe forgiveness is necessary for the health of our world. Blessings on all the ways we can find ourselves traveling to that place of peace.

Reflection Questions and Journal Prompts

- *What does this story evoke in you?*

- *Do you notice relationships in your life where resentment is causing a separation or sadness, anger or suffering on your part? How does this live in your body? How does this affect your emotion self? What is your mind's process around this? How does it influence your relationships?*

- *Do you find yourself judging yourself for having resentment? Have you tried forgiving and feel disappointment that it didn't resolve anything for you? Have you tried to jump over the small self's need to express itself with the hope of landing in the Higher Self, only to discover that doesn't work for you?*

- *Is part of you reluctant to forgive? What does that part of you believe it gains by hanging on to the resentment?*

- *What would it take for you to be willing to let this go?*

- *Can you speak to relationship healing in your life where you have been able to forgive and let go of suffering? What helped you to do that?*

- *Are there self-resentments, shame or guilt that you carry against yourself? What has stopped you from releasing them or letting them go? What is this costing you?*

- *Have there been situations where you have erred or missed the mark and you were able to extend forgiveness to yourself? What helped you get there? How is this different from places where you may not yet have been able to let go into self-forgiveness?*

- *Spend some time, if you are willing, noticing the power of forgiveness in your life. Be with your own stories of forgiveness and letting go. Do you have a favorite way of releasing resentment?*

- *Is there an issue of resentment with yourself or another, with which you would be willing to open to the possibility of forgiveness? What or whom could you welcome that would assist you with this?*

Meditation on Forgiveness

Begin by finding a place to relax where you won't be disturbed. Invite your body to relax. Let your breath bring a softening to every muscle, every organ, and every cell of your body. Let your breath bring a gift of relaxation to your emotion self. Let the breath also bring a sense of peace to the mind. In this place of welcoming relaxation and peace there is nothing to do. There is nothing to force. There is only welcoming and allowing of relaxation and peace.

In this deep place of relaxation, you allow yourself to go to a safe place where you are able to move even deeper into peace and relaxation. As you find yourself in this safe place you notice how your body loves it here. How the temperature and air is just right for you. You notice how the sights and sounds enhance your sense of peace and safety. All is a magnificent match for your deep relaxation and peace.

In this place, you may now choose to remain here and spend this time breathing deeply in this peace and relaxation. You may also choose to journey with this peace and relaxation in a process of forgiving something you have been carrying with yourself or with another.

If you are choosing to journey in forgiveness, you now notice that in the distance there is a guide or helper who begins to come toward you. This helper is smiling at you and encouraging you to welcome more freedom in your life by entering a forgiveness process. The guide or helper asks whether at this time you are wishing to release resentment with yourself or someone else. The helper asks which issue it is that you are ready to release, reminding you not to try to forgive everything at once.

Once there is clarity about who and what you are ready to forgive, your helper begins to walk with you toward a place that is spacious enough to hold all your feelings and reactions about this issue. In this place you find all that you need to empty out your suffering. You find all the physical things you need. You find all the energy of love, compassion and acceptance that you need. You find all the support you need. And you find all the guidance that you need. You find all that you need now to first honor your suffering and then to let go, to release, to find your way through your pain to forgiveness. You have all the time, space and support that you need for your very real human self to release and empty out its suffering. And then you are able to rise beyond this human aspect of you to the Highest Self of you that carries compassion and the ability to forgive. It is from this place that the essence of you is able to extend forgiveness to this other person or to yourself.

The forgiving is filled with love for all that you are and all that others are. The forgiving energy reminds you that there may be amends to make, but this reminder comes not with judgment, but with acceptance. The forgiving energy reminds you that this does not require you to give up healthy boundaries. You do not need to continue a relationship with another that is not healthy for you. And this forgiving energy guides you in finding a way to feel at least neutral, if not loving, toward the other who has hurt you or to yourself for the place you have missed the mark. Whatever is called for unfolds for you in perfect harmony. Whatever amount of healing that unfolds is known, in the depths of your bones, to be just perfect for now. There is no judgment, no expectation of how this needs to be. There is only what is just right for you now.

If you notice any judgment with yourself about this journey, your guide quickly and easily helps you to transform that energy to the energy of love. It is in this energy of love that you now take time to rest and integrate what has taken place. You may feel that this is complete. You may feel that it is the beginning of a process for you. You may have received the gift of knowing what is impeding your forgiveness. Perhaps you have received the knowing that you would like to welcome some ongoing support with forgiveness in your life. Whatever you have received, you trust that it is just right for you in this time and place. And you give gratitude for what has transpired.

Your helper gazes at you with unconditional love and honoring as you walk together to the place where you first began this journey of forgiveness. With each step of this return, you feel yourself integrating all that has transpired. As you arrive back at the beginning place of this journey, you thank your helper who offers you any last words of wisdom and support. Perhaps you agree to meet again. When this feels complete, you say goodbye.

And now, whether you have been in this original place of safety resting in peace and relaxation, or have been journeying in forgiveness, you begin to complete your time in this place. You give thanks for everything and begin to bring your consciousness back to the original place where you began to relax. You notice the surface that supports your body. You notice the temperature in the room or environment. You notice any sounds around you. You notice your breath. You take a couple of comfortably deep breaths and when you are ready you open your eyes. You give yourself all the time you need to reorient to this time and place.

When you are ready, you may wish to journal about your experience. You may wish to seek out new resources on forgiveness. You may wish to seek out a trusted friend or companion, a therapist, spiritual director, or other helper with whom to process or to accompany you in the ongoing spiritual practice of forgiveness.

UNBRIDLED JOY

I sat on that old Shetland pony, the one that never, ever went anywhere no matter how many "giddy-ups" and heels in the side he received. Time after time I would sit on his chubby little body with my childhood chubby little body and that was it. We just sat there.

It is true that we never actually went anywhere, but one day sitting on him I had a fantasy of miraculous transformation. That day I imagined that I would get up on him as usual and settle in to have a good sit, to go nowhere. And without so much as one giddy-up, without so much as a gentle nudge, with no warning at all, he would throw off his bridle and off we would go at break neck speed. I would hang on to his mane, and we would fly out of the pasture and over the open spaces that would zoom by in a blur. My hair would blow in the wind, I would laugh uncontrollably, and I am pretty sure that in my fantasy, the pony would be laughing too.

Unbridled joy. When we are present to what is, even if it is a pony going nowhere, we just might be opened up to something more. It is in this opening that we can access our joy. Running through the sprinkler on a hot August day, tickling and being tickled, eating marshmallow treats in the living room when *The Wizard of Oz* was on, and chasing Fourth of July parachutes across our farm fields and pastures, were some of my places of unbridled joy as a child.

I had the great fortune to meet my friend Sarah while we were both attending graduate school. Such unbridled joy we had. We made up game shows with goofy shared class experiences, such as "Let's have Scandalous Behaviors on the D.C. Travel Seminar, for five hundred, Alex." We had even goofier nicknames for all our instructors, like *Natalie-Massive-Earrings-Jones*. This kind of crazy, laugh-until-you-cry, nearly wet-your-pants, joy carried us through a lot of stress. Even today when we get together we can't help ourselves—we laugh hysterically in no time at all.

Family photos where someone sports rabbit ears still bring me great childish joy. Bare feet on the warm earth, splashing in the ocean and the dolphins coming up to the Gulf of Mexico shoreline to swim with me are memories of unabashed joy. The first song of the redwing blackbird in the Midwest springtime, and the squawking of the desert Gambel's quail in awkward flight always make my heart fill with joy. The last melting of the Midwest winter's snow leaves me giddy. I have had to pull over more than once while listening to the "Lake Wobegone Stories" on CD in my car because my bubbling-up laughter was risking my safety and that of other drivers. Calling my partner the newest nicknames and terms of endearment leave me smiling until my face hurts. And there is really nothing to compare with the sound of children's laughter, especially my three- and five-year-old buddies.

Now that's the music of joy.

Sometimes there's a quieter, yet still unbridled, joy, like when I am in Arizona in March and the sunset casts its soft mauve glow on the face of the Santa Catalina Mountains. In my work with clients there is surprising, unbridled, wondrous joy. People have told me that they are surprised to hear laughter coming from my office, but I think that because we are opening ourselves up to our deepest sorrows, we are also opening up to our deepest joys. I remember sitting with a woman who felt her mother criticized everything about her.

She recited item after item on the list of ways she felt she had disappointed her mother. Then she got to, "My handwriting is even too big!"

Suddenly our eyes got wide and we looked at each other for a silent moment before both of us, at the very same instant, began to laugh. We choked and sputtered until tears ran down our cheeks. Joy can take us to the bigger picture; can shift our perspective, as it did for this woman.

Even as I am writing this, I feel joy just bubbling up inside me, uncontainable like the bubbles in sparkling wine or a childhood bubble bath. Wouldn't it be great if we could bottle our joy and pour its concentrate into our exhaled breath, just like we pour bubble bath under the faucet? The breath would make contact with the joy concentrate and just bubble, overflow and spread out everywhere. Our very cells would feel like dancing, and those around us couldn't escape the spread of our joy.

There are many benefits to harvesting and collecting our joy. Being open to joy, welcoming joy each day and revisiting joyful memories enhances our physical health. I am sure it enhances our emotional health, too, especially since it's hard to hold a lot of needless mental chatter while in the midst of a joy fix. I believe that when we are in our most expansive Self, joy, along with unconditional love and compassion live right there with us.

Even when we are aware of our own suffering, the suffering of others and global suffering, if we hold our joy near us, in our deepest heart pocket, it won't fall out.

Reflection Questions and Journal Prompts

- *What are your joy stories?*

- *Has what brings you joy changed over time? If so, what is your understanding of that shift?*

- *How does joy connect you to places, people and yourself?*

- *How do you notice the effect of joy in your body? In your emotion self? In your thinking mind? In the very spirit of you?*

- *What might you say about how joy opens you up to more possibility and transformation in your life? Can you share examples of this?*

Suggested Activities or Experiences

- *You might draw, sculpt, or write a poem about joy.*

- *You might put on a piece of music that speaks of joy and allow your mind/body/spirit to move in joy to that music.*

- *You might make a magical joy pouch and symbolically place all your joy memories gathered so far into that pouch. This magical pouch expands mysteriously to hold the full magnitude of joy you wish to carry. You might carry this over your heart. You might find it comforting to hold this pouch when you experience sadness, sorrow or pain. The pouch can remind you that you can hold both joy and other emotions, too. The pouch might remind you that the joy is right there with you, even if you can't feel it.*

- *You could enter a day with the intention that you are a magnet for joy and then just notice all the joyful experiences to be had. You could begin a practice of making a standing joy date with yourself each week.*

Meditation on Joy

Find a place where you can sit or lie down and be uninterrupted for a few minutes. Begin this quiet time by noticing your breath, noticing the experience of your body, the experience of your emotion self, the experience of your mind. Just notice with loving awareness. No judgment. No need to change anything. No forcing or effort to be or experience anything other than who you are and what you are experiencing.

After a few quiet moments, allow yourself an inner journey of joy. Find yourself transported to a place where you remember or discover great joy. This is a place that is just right for you and you allow yourself to be present there. This place, just by its environment brings joy to all your senses. The visual images here are joyful. Any particular scents or fragrances are joyful for you. The temperature and the weather joyfully match your desires. The sounds present fill you with joy. You notice your perfect joyful place and you take it in with all your senses.

While your senses are fully happy, there is still more here for you. You begin to notice that your desire to be alone here or with others immediately materializes. Whether alone or with the others of your choosing, you find that there is an area that holds many items that stir joy for you. Perhaps there are art supplies. Perhaps there are bubbles. Perhaps there are photos. Perhaps there are magic wands to transport you to the destination of your choice. Whatever is in this area is just right for you.

What unfolds now is also just right for you. Perhaps you enter an activity with the items gathered. Perhaps you travel to a special place. Perhaps you take a journey down memory lane and re-collect your joy memories. Perhaps you find yourself spontaneously making new joy memories. You find yourself expanding to feel more joy than ever and you experience this expansive joy in every fiber of your being. You notice how your body, emotion, mind and spirit respond to this joy. You notice the freedom this brings. You take all the time you need to live in this joy in new and amplified ways.

Before you return to where this meditation first began, you find a symbol, object, word or some reminder to take with you as a way of

210

remembering your deep capacity for joy. This is something that you can carry with you through your days, a joy talisman of sorts.

With your joy talisman you return now to the place where you first began this meditation. You take comfortably deep breaths and open your eyes when you are ready. You notice how you feel, the same or different as when you began this meditation. There is no right or wrong, just notice. You give gratitude for whatever has unfolded and you take all the time you need to integrate your experience.

You may wish to journal or share your experience with a friend.

THE ILLUSION OF DIFFERENCE

Up from the basement he would come with his noisy, lop-sided gait, laughing and asking for paper money. He would often wait for a ride out to the farm where he loved the chores he could do. When he rested, he would thumb through his worn car and truck magazines looking for the GMCs.

I never knew what mood she would be dressed in on those rare moments she emerged from her bedroom. Would she be sullen, grumpy and uttering words I was unable to understand? Would she be silent and glowering? Would she be just silent?

When I was really young, Aunt Bernice seemed scary and I didn't know how to communicate with her. I yearned to relate to Uncle Warren in ways beyond car and truck magazines and paper money.

It was painful to hear others making disparaging remarks about them. "Mentally retarded," "developmentally disabled," "differently abled." Whatever you called it, growing up with Uncle Warren and Aunt Bernice had its challenges, but there was something that united us. We were family and being family meant that, regardless of our differences, we belonged to each other.

Years later, when my ill and aging grandparents could no longer care for them, they found surprising happiness and like-minded community when a new group home in a nearby town opened. Here they could partake in activities and sheltered workshop jobs, things beyond what my dedicated and loving grandparents could provide.

My Aunt Bernice and Uncle Warren progressed in language and social skills in a way that made us all proud. The sullenness that had seemed to ooze from Bernice in earlier years was gone and her smile was a delight. Warren never lost his love of going to the farm nor asking for paper money. They found an additional family to which they belonged.

≈

When I was about ten years old, I remember being upstairs in my room and hearing my dad's raised voice below as he told my brother he had to get them back. I couldn't imagine what this was about, but knew it must be important because my dad rarely raised his voice. I later found out that my eight-year-old brother then explained to dad that he had given his shoes away to a younger boy. The boy, who was dressed in raggedy clothes and was barefoot, told my brother that he had outgrown his shoes and his family didn't have the money to replace them. My brother, recognizing the boy's plight and putting himself in his shoes (pun intended), saw the boy as a fellow human who, like us all, just needed a little extra help and kindness. Those shoes did not return to our house. My brother had recognized the larger sense of family to which we belong.

My first job after college was a house parent at a girl's group home. Two of us rotated living there three and a half days each week. When I started, I was petrified. I was only twenty-two years old and responsible for eight adolescent girls who had been placed out of their homes for a variety of reasons. To make matters worse, the supervisor was going on vacation.

When I expressed my concerns, she said that one of the nuns in an adjoining building of the campus would be available to guide me if I had questions. But when I met the kind and good-hearted Sister, I could not understand a word she was saying. She had left China many years before, but English remained a challenge.

That first weekend on the job, I was on my own when one girl ran away and another came home from a scheduled evening out drunk and puking. I still wonder how I lasted two and a half years at that job, but before I left, I'd come to love those girls as if they were my own. Sister and I learned to communicate less by language and more through shared mutual respect and I acquired the ability to understand about every third word she spoke.

I have had the great gift to journey in this life with other people who at first glance seem very different from me. Our natural instinct may be to fear others who appear different, as I once feared my Aunt Bernice. Our fear can manifest in many ways.

We may try to keep ourselves separate, puff up with our own sense of superiority, or deny certain rights to this group or that.

We may build walls or rationalize our discrimination in lots of creative ways. But this way of seeing is limiting and an illusion. If we take time to know each other, regardless of our skin color, religion or spiritual tradition, income bracket, age, nationality, intellect, social skills, gender, sexual orientation, or any number of other diversities, we will find that great Heart of the Oneness that beats in us all. We will remember that we belong to each other. We will remember that we are all family.

Reflection Questions and Journal Prompts

- *What, if anything, touches you in these stories?*

- *What are your own stories of differences? Do you have stories of being with others who are perceived as different? Do you have stories of being the one who is perceived as different?*

- *Where have you found yourself moving beyond a sense of difference?*

- *Have there been places, or are there still places, where it is challenging to get beyond what appears different? If so, which places of difference are most difficult for you?*

- *What do you notice about your own inner process and your behavior when you perceive difference?*

- *Are there any places here where you are welcoming a shift in perception? Why or why not? Are there places where you have remembered the larger sense of family? If so, what does that larger sense of family mean to you?*

Suggested Activities or Experiences

- *You might identify a place in your life where it is difficult to accept someone perceived as different from you. Perhaps this person is a different gender, has a different sexual orientation, or is from a different culture. Or, maybe this person holds a different political view from you on a topic near and dear to your heart.*

- *You could then imagine regarding this person from your ego self and focus on the differences between you.*

- *Then you might allow yourself time and space to intentionally center in your Highest Consciousness Self. From this larger perspective, see if you can honor the places where you do not appear the same and see if you might find some common ground.*

- *Share this experience with a friend or companion or, you might wish to journal about what this was like for you. Try to suspend judgment and just explore your own process around differences and similarities.*

- *Spend a day intentionally moving in the world as your ego or personality self and notice issues of difference or similarity.*

- *Spend a day intentionally moving in the world as your Highest Consciousness Self and notice issues of similarity. How, if at all, are these two ways of moving in the world the same or different?*

- *What tools or practices help you to get beyond differences?*

CINDY CHICOINE

A note about the following meditation . . .

The Buddha's words on Loving-Kindness are called the Metta Sutra. A practice for developing loving-kindness and goodwill toward others had been called Metta or Ton Glen by author Pema Chodron and others. This practice helps us focus beneath our differences to what is the same in all of us—the desire for happiness, to be treated with respect and kindness. In this practice we send loving-kindness first to ourselves, then a good friend, a neutral person, a difficult person and finally, to all beings.

Meditation on Loving-Kindness

(A Variation on the Buddhist Practice of Ton Glen or Metta)

Find a place to sit where you will not be disturbed. Close your eyes if that is comfortable for you. Take time to center into your own self. Take time to breathe and center. There is no rushing or hurrying. There is no effort or forcing. There is only the willingness to explore this kind of meditation.

When you are ready with your eyes closed, if that is comfortable for you, imagine your own heart is bright, like the sun. Breathe into your heart center until your own heart light glows with the same intensity of light as the sun.

When you feel anchored in the strength of your own heart light, imagine sitting across from the image of yourself. You notice any darkness or suffering around the heart of that image of yourself.

With heart bright as the sun, you breathe in any of that darkness that exists around the heart of yourself. You do not breathe this into the lungs.

You breathe the darkness into that vibrant heart light. In the vibrant heart light, the darkness, as soon as it hits the bright light, dissipates and disappears. (This is just like a cloud that hits the sun and is instantly gone.)

With each breath of darkness that you breathe from yourself, you breathe back loving-kindness. As you breathe back love, you notice that the heart light just keeps getting brighter and brighter. Breathing in the darkness and breathing back love makes the heart light even stronger and brighter.

You continue this practice until the darkness around the heart of your self has disappeared. You then release the image of yourself sitting across from you.

Then, imagine a dear friend or loved one sitting across from you. Once again, you center in the brightness of the heart light. Then you notice any darkness or suffering around the friend or loved one. You offer this same practice to them. You breathe the darkness into the heart light where it disappears and you breathe back loving-kindness.

When this feels complete, you release the image of this person.

You next imagine sitting across from you is someone with whom you neither feel like nor dislike. And for this neutral person you breathe in any suffering or darkness around them into the heart light that is bright like the sun. The darkness instantly disappears when it makes contact with the bright light of the heart and you breathe back loving-kindness.

When this feels complete you release the image of this person.

Next you imagine someone with whom you disagree, an enemy, or someone you perceive as different in a way that is difficult for you. And you follow the same practice of noticing any darkness, breathing any suffering or darkness into the heart light and breathing back loving-kindness.

When this feels complete, you release the image of this person.

You now see across from you an image that is representative of all beings everywhere. You offer loving-kindness to all beings, breathing any suffering into the heart light and breathing back the energy of loving-kindness.

When this feels complete, you release this image.

You end by breathing once more in and out of your own heart center and with each breath your heart light is strong and bright.

You give gratitude for this experience. You give gratitude for all who have offered themselves for this practice of loving-kindness, metta or ton glen.

You open your eyes when you are ready and allow time to integrate your experience.

You may wish to process your experience with a friend or companion. You may also wish to journal about it.

AUTOGRAPHS OF THE BODY

My grade school, blue vinyl-covered autograph book with its plain, stark white paper held warm new meaning as it was passed among my classmates. Their names and simple words written in their own hand became in some way a small anchor of the grade school chapter of my life.

The plain white paper napkin was transformed when Leonardo DiCaprio moved through that Iowa diner one day. Kind and generous in his greeting of the customers, he stopped to sign his name in a way that gave life to something that only moments before was intended to wipe the dribbles of mustard from my hand or chin.

A painting party of a large canvas labyrinth left sprinkles and blobs of purple paint scattered here and there. Some called those splotches "mistakes." I named them "autographs," memories of those on their knees for hours donating love and energy to mark the path.

The skin of elk stretched taut around the wooden drum frame. Once I moved beyond the gamey smell and slimy texture, the animal's signature was unmistakable. The stretch marks and scars, the thick places and thin—almost translucent—places all drew me in and began a time of wondering about life given, and still living, in that powerful drum.

An autograph, according to the New American Webster dictionary, is "one's own signature." And now, the autographs rise up to be acknowledged by this body of mine, this spirit infused flesh.

There are invisible signatures, like the mended bone in my left arm from an overzealous jump out of the childhood swing set, and the torn cartilage in one knee from my last volleyball game. There are nearly invisible signatures, like the slightly off gait left behind after the infant and toddler foot casts that re-formed my feet, and the creaky-neck stiffness from whiplash experienced years ago. There are visible signatures for anyone who looks closely, some subtle like the scar on my knee from a childhood fall and others more obvious, like the wrinkles from aging and from many rays of sunshine drawn into my eager, upturned face. And there are signatures visible to a select few, like my own stretch marks from a lifetime of shifting weight, the torn muscle in my back from nautilus sessions with a poorly trained instructor, and the scarring left by a tender and skilled surgeon removing breast cancer in a lumpectomy. This fifty-year plus body has stories to tell.

Some cultures scar, stretch and mark their bodies in rituals and ceremonies of belonging and transition. My autographs, my own body signatures, weren't consciously given for belonging and transition, but my body does claim belonging—to play, athletics, accident recovery, and more. My body does claim transition—from breast cancer patient to breast cancer survivor, and more.

Once we can move past whatever might repel us, we can go deeper and acknowledge the story. The Holy has given me a life of spirit-infused flesh but it is in the stories of that flesh that life and spirit live on. This was never clearer than when my sister-in-law was dying of breast cancer.

Hospice support made it possible for her to be at home surrounded by her husband, sons and those of us who loved her. Hours before her death, a few of us gathered to bless her body. We were guided by the deep compassion, wisdom and physical presence of Joyce Rupp, who later wrote of this special blessing time, "The Blessing of One Who Draws Near Death" in her book, *Out of the Ordinary.*

Joyce guided as we touched parts of Jane's body as remembrances were shared. "Thank you for your questioning and your wisdom-filled mind," shared a friend. "Mom, thank you for these feet and legs that took us skiing and ice skating," said her son. Eyes, ears, hands, all were blessed as we acknowledged the body that held her spirit and the stories that body held. With this we sent her forth for her journey home.

I hope that one day my body might be similarly blessed with such heartfelt reverence. Life given and living on through body stories. My own unique visible and invisible autographs and signatures: kneeling in religious buildings and holy gardens, body of turning and whirling in Dances of Universal Peace circles, hands of spirit-guided holding, eyes flowing with tears of love, trail and labyrinth walking feet, large heart, full-bodied hugs, skin warmed by Spirit-given sun.

Oh, yes, these bodies have stories to tell.

Reflection Questions and Journal Prompts

- *What stands out for you in this story?*

- *Like the autographed napkin, are you aware of something in your life whose meaning has been changed or transformed from the ordinary to something more?*

- *What are your body's autographs and unique signatures?*

- *Where are you in the journey of loving and accepting these autographs rather than judging and criticizing?*

- *What stories of your spirit-infused flesh are waiting to be told?*

- *In what ways might these body stories speak of belonging? In what ways might they speak of your transition places?*

- *Would you invite a blessing of your body as you near death? Why, or why not? If you did welcome a final blessing, what might that look and feel like? What rituals would you like to be a part of this blessing? What stories would you want to be told?*

Meditation on Your Body's Final Blessing

Find a comfortable place to sit or lie down where you won't be interrupted. Begin by noticing your breath. Allow the breath to bring you to a place of safety and relaxation. Find yourself softening and opening with each breath. Nothing to force. No effort. Just breathing, softening and opening.

When you are ready, allow yourself to travel to a place of safety where you will be blessed. Perhaps you will find yourself in a favorite room of your home. Perhaps you will be in nature. Perhaps you will find another place altogether. Trust yourself to know.

In this safe place, become aware of the sounds, tastes, smells, temperature and any other sensory awareness. You have the ability to make this a safe sensory place for you, and so you fine tune anything that will make it be just right.

You also have the ability to gather all those whom you wish to have at this final blessing of your body on the earth. You may gather family and friends. You may have mind/body/spirit helpers present. There may be living ancestors, or perhaps those who have gone beyond, with you. You may invite anyone who would be of comfort to you and whom you wish to witness you. Once again, trust yourself to know.

As you prepare for this final blessing, you are able to ask for and receive anything you wish for before the blessings begin. Those present are also readying themselves for this sacred blessing time. Whatever ritual surrounds this it is by your design. Perhaps there is sacred oil that is touched on each area of your body as memories and stories are shared.

Perhaps your loved ones just gently touch each area of your body as it is blessed.

Perhaps you wish those gathered to merely gesture to each body area.

Perhaps sacred readings or poetry is shared.

Perhaps music.

Maybe there are candles or other ritual elements. See it unfold in the perfect way for you and those gathered. Amazingly you listen and receive the perfect blessing. You hear those stories you had so hoped would be shared by those you hoped would share them. You trust the perfect stories will live on after your passing. You feel loved and honored and receive all that you need to make this final transition.

Stay with your experience as it unfolds perfectly for as long as feels just right for you and until a perfect completion is found.

Then begin to return to ordinary consciousness by noticing the air in the room where you began this meditation. Feel your body in contact with the surface that supports it. Notice any sounds in the room. Let your breath be deep and full and open your eyes. Give yourself plenty of time to re-enter this current time and place.

Journal, if you wish, about your experience. Take particular note of anything you may wish to begin to put in place now for a future blessing time for you. Notice if you feel called to share this experience with someone.

DANA: BEYOND ENDURING TO FLOURISHING

"Dana" is a name for primordial power or life force by the Celtic people. Dana is Spirit. Dana is everywhere, in everything. Trees, the earth, spirit helpers, all pulse with Dana spirit. This wider energy of the universe, this energy of transformation, has been called many things by many cultures, the Tao or Chi in the Chinese tradition, or Holy Spirit in the Christian tradition for example.

Several years ago on a visit to California, it felt as if I was welcomed into John Muir Woods by the trees. Walking the path shared by ancient and giant redwoods was mind and spirit expanding. One particular redwood drew me in, literally in, to her. She had a giant cave-like hole in her trunk extending from the floor of the forest up about ten or fifteen feet. It was as if a magnetic force drew me into her womb.

I stood inside her transfixed, hypnotized, at one with her and with everything. As I breathed, I felt a glow of aliveness and grace all over my being and felt I was breathing with her and the entire Universe.

At some point, I became aware that the inside wall of this womb was black and charred. I was shocked to realize she had been on fire. How could I feel such vibrancy and life inside something that must clearly be dead from fire?

I exited her womb on unsteady legs and with sadness. I looked up, expecting to see dry, dead branches and was surprised to see vibrant growth way up to the very top. Surprise and relief washed over me. I don't know how long I was with her but I felt so at home and in kinship with her that it was hard to pull away.

Further along the path was a sign that told of the relationship of fire to the redwood. Fire does not always destroy these trees. For the tree that survives the fire, it lives to see its seeds are cracked open by the heat resulting in new trees scattered all around. This was Dana in action—an undeniable force, a transformational energy that heals, that breaks down in order to allow, even invite, a breaking through and new life.

We are all hollowed out by life sometimes. When I journeyed through breast cancer treatment, climbed a trail that seemed destined to tumble me down the steep bluff, witnessed my beloved father die, or had my heart wounded by a changing relationship, I was hollowed out. But if we can surrender, in spite of our fears, to the greater transformational energies meeting us during these difficult times, we can come to a place where there is no longer a sense of just enduring the problem or just getting through it the best we can. We can be purged of what needs to be released, be hollowed out to create a womb that gestates new shoots of life that can reach even farther than before, reaching to the depths of our Spirit-given, vibrant wisdom.

Redwoods thriving through fire have it. I have it. You have it too. Let's welcome it in. Let's invite it to live with us. Let's scatter the fresh growth of Dana.

Reflection Questions and Journal Prompts

- *Where are the places in your life, or the experiences of your life, where you have been "hollowed out"?*

- *How would you describe that experience of hollowing, or that place of surrender?*

- *In this hollowing, what were you pushed to purge or release? What was that process like for you?*

- *Can you relate to the hollowing process creating a womb in you, a place that gestated new life? What can you claim about that new life?*

- *Where are you aware of the presence of Dana in your world? What signs of this Dana presence exist in your beingness?*

Meditation with Dana

Find a place where you can sit or lie down and be uninterrupted for a few minutes. Begin this quiet time by noticing your breath, noticing the experience of your body, the experience of your emotion self, the experience of your mind. Just notice with loving awareness. No judgment. No need to change anything. No forcing or effort to be or experience anything other than who you are and what you are experiencing.

After a few quiet moments, allow yourself an inner journey in nature. Find yourself outside in a place that is just right for you. Perhaps you journey to an island with soft, warm ocean breezes. Perhaps, you find yourself in a meadow with the springtime sun, or snowshoeing in a north-wood trail. Just allow yourself to go to the place that is perfect for you on this day.

In your nature place, allow yourself to notice the visual images all around you. Allow yourself to notice any particular pleasing scents. You also notice that the temperature and weather is just perfect for you. The sounds are pleasing and you take in this place with all of your senses.

In this nature place of your choosing, you allow yourself to pause in the quiet stillness of this place. You find yourself opening to the experience of the life force of this place, the Dana spirit.

You may be called to stand, sit or lie down in a particular place here as your awareness of Dana continues to open up. Or you may be called to walk or move in a way that you seek out, soak up or immerse yourself in Dana. Whatever is your way, you invite the Dana of this place to reveal itself to you.

You notice how you experience this life force energy called Dana. Perhaps you feel it in the rising hair on your arms. Perhaps you tingle inside with inner goose bumps. Perhaps it is felt as overflowing joy in your heart.

Perhaps it offers itself as a quieting of your mind.

Perhaps it makes itself known as a deep kind of knowing within.

Whatever way it is experienced, you allow yourself to be present to it. You also find yourself aware of that same Dana presence inside you, in addition to being around you. It may be a familiar sensation or experience. It may be surprising. But, it is unmistakable. Dana lives inside you, too.

You allow yourself the time and space to join your Dana with the Dana in your nature place. You take all the time you need to allow this merging, this union, and this partnership.

You anchor your experience with Dana deep inside yourself, deep inside your bones, and in every cell and fiber of your being. You know that you can draw upon this energy whenever you need it. You know that you can be with it in every moment of your life.

As you begin now to return to the original place where you began this meditation, you notice your breath, the temperature and any sounds around you. You notice your body and whatever floor, chair or surface is supporting it. You bring your full consciousness and awareness back into this present moment and the place where you first began this meditation. Before you enter the next chapter of your day, you allow yourself some moments of transition. You can take whatever gifts you have just experienced into the next part of your day.

You may wish to share your experience with someone or journal about it.

TURNING AROUND THE HEART

A few years ago, our local Dances of Universal Peace group invited a Sufi woman to come to our city and share the wisdom of Jelaluddin Rumi, the mystic, Sufi poet born in 1207. It was a day of music, movement, poetry and reflection, all things I love. What I didn't realize was an even greater gift than enjoying those beautiful things was to come out of that day.

Late in the day, our guest shared this story from Rumi's life. One evening, Rumi's cook, burned his foot in the fire while preparing Rumi's dinner. As he brought the dinner to Rumi, he thought the burned foot was ugly and a disgrace so he stood with the toes of one foot over the other trying to hide the injury.

Rumi, noticing this odd posture, asked the man what was going on. He confessed his perceived disgrace and its cause.

Rumi arose from his seated position and assumed the same pose of one foot over the other. He spoke kindly of the man's service and of the goodness of his heart. He told the man to release his embarrassment, that his feet were beautiful and of the Beloved. And from that position, of one foot over the other, Rumi began to turn to his left, turning faster and faster, until he was one with the Beloved, Rumi's name for God, or Allah.

Our guest went on to share that the Sufi "turning," or what we often refer to as "whirling," began at that time. She also told us that when the Sufi turns, they are turning around the altar of the heart, the residence of the Beloved in us. They turn with one hand raised to the heavens and the other hand toward the earth, as they bring down the blessings of the Beloved. The blessings move through the dervish and are offered to the earth. The dervish becomes a conduit of the sacred energies of the Beloved and turns around the heart until the dervish *becomes* the holy and transcends the ego self. Another aspect of this turning, as she explained, is that this movement clears and brushes clean the heart, removing anything that separates us from the felt sense of the Divine.

This story is powerful to me on many levels. I was born with my feet turned in, which is often called "pigeon-toed." To correct this, I had my feet cast in plaster as an infant then later wore orthotic shoes. At a time when kids were wearing cool shoes, there were no *PF Flyers* for me. I felt left out and embarrassed. Today my feet are fine and I am grateful to all those interventions that I may walk, yet at the time it was something that just seemed to set me apart.

I am also one who has always been a heart person, sensing and feeling the energies and emotions of others. This meant I was frequently in tears, tears of joy and being moved by love, tears of sadness, and sometimes tears of anger.

As a child, I was often accused of being too sensitive and emotional. While I have come to understand sensitivity as a gift, at the time it was, like my pigeon toes, another thing that made me separate from others. When I heard the Sufi story of toes turned inward and turning around the altar of that heart, my own heart felt cleansed of any remaining self-consciousness of those two connected areas of my youth. I felt like I was home.

If our day with the Sufi teacher had ended right there, I would have felt supremely gifted. But there was more to come. We were offered the chance to learn how to turn, to move around the altar of our heart, to move beyond the ego into union with the Beloved.

I was scared. I wanted so badly to do this, and yet my inner critic was speaking loudly, "You aren't athletic. You'll lose your balance. You aren't a dancer. You had better pass because you can't do this. You'll make a fool of yourself."

And yet, a deeper voice arose in me. It said, "This *is* for you. Your feet are not a disgrace; they are of the holy. Perhaps you were born to turn. Your heart is an altar, and through this holy place you can connect with the Beloved. You can do it."

As the Sufi teacher taught us how to turn, I listened with rapture, trust and just a pinch of fear.

"Okay," she said, "let's stand with our feet turned in and give it a try."

The music played. Slowly at first, I began to turn . . . round and round, then faster and faster, until I found myself moving with grace and speed and felt myself dissolving into the great beyond, losing all self-consciousness, releasing all worry, maintaining a balance rarely felt in the movement of my life. I was turning. I was a conduit of the Presence. I was love, pure and simple love.

There are many ways to be an instrument of the Holy. There are many ways, taught by many spiritual traditions, to transcend the ego self. There are many ways to overcome fear and move beyond old perceptions of ourselves.

And on that day, I was given two gifts: One was reinforcement of the belief that my heart and sensitivity are strengths rather than weaknesses and the other was the opportunity to view my feet as something that can offer inclusion rather than separation.

While you won't find me on the ball fields, or cycling down mountains, or jogging along city streets, if you come upon a whirling dervish, look closely. It just might be me.

The Secret of Turning

A secret turning in us
makes the universe turn.
Head unaware of feet,
and feet head. Neither cares.
They keep turning.
Jelaluddin Rumi

Translated/Compiled by Coleman Barks.
The Essential Rumi. Harper San Francisco, 1997

Reflection Questions and Journal Prompts

- *What, if anything, speaks to you from this story?*

- *Can you speak to places of insecurity or embarrassment in your own life? Have you been able to later see the gift in these things?*

- *How have you, in your own life, overcome fear or old ways of perceiving yourself?*

- *Can you relate to the inner voices of both the critic and the wiser Self? Where some are places in your own life that you notice this inner dialogue?*

- *The Sufis believe the Beloved lives in the heart of the human self. Do you have a sense of where the Holy lives in your body? Would this, or does this, impact the way you care for your body?*

- *What are ways that you transcend the ego or critic self, and become a conduit of the Divine Presence? What ways do you bring gifts through you and into our world?*

Suggested Activities or Experiences

- *You might pick an area of your life where you hear competing voices, like the inner critic and the wise Self, and actually write out the dialogue or speak it aloud. If you enter into this experience, you may wish to give your wise Self the last comments.*

- *You might write about or create an artistic expression of an old perception of yourself and how this has transformed over time.*

- *Imagine your heart as the altar, the residence of the Divine, inside you. Create a physical expression of this altar with clay, paint, drawing, poetry or movement. What divine qualities live in the altar of your heart? Just notice how your life flows when you are in contact with, turning around the heart of, those qualities.*

- *Seek out a Sufi gathering where you may be able to witness the turning of the dervishes. Perhaps you can find a class or workshop offered where you might be able to learn to turn.*

- *You might spend a day moving in the world in a way where you are conscious of keeping your heart "polished," or clear for the Holy to reside there. Just notice what that is like for you. Perhaps you'll find you want to continue this practice for a longer time.*

- *You might seek out at least one additional practice or experience that can assist you in transcending the smaller self to claim your Self as an expression of the Beloved.*

Meditation on Turning Around the Heart

Find a comfortable place to sit or lie down where you won't be disturbed. Close your eyes if that is comfortable for you. Allow your awareness to come to your breath. For now, just notice the breath.

In and out, in and out. Let the breath breathe you. Be breathed by the breath. Take all the time you need right now to just be with the breath.

And when you are ready, you welcome your body into this day, into this experience. Begin by bringing loving awareness to the body. Just notice how the body is at this moment of the day. There is no need to change anything and there is no judgment, only loving awareness of the body.

Notice any places of tension, discomfort or holding.

Notice any places of ease, flow and comfort in the body. Welcome the body into this experience, this day and breathe a breath of acceptance to the body. Only after extending awareness, welcome and acceptance to the body do you notice if there is any tension, holding or energy in the body, that is no longer needed, that is ready to be released. If so, then you just let it go, perhaps sailing it out on the exhaled breath. And if this created any new spaciousness in the body, you can use your breath to expand out the health and wholeness that lives at your core into this newly opened space.

You may also wish to partner that with breathing in the wholeness energy available in the larger universe outside of you. Breathing in, and expanding out health and wholeness for the body.

You can extend this same welcome to the emotion self. Begin by noticing with loving awareness whatever emotions are present with you this moment of this day. No judgment, no right or wrong, no need to change anything. For now just notice the emotion self. Welcome the emotion self into this day.

When you are ready, breathe a breath of acceptance to the emotion self no matter what is found there. And only after this welcoming and this extending of acceptance do you notice if there is any emotion energy that is no longer needed that is ready to be released. And if there is, you just let it go. Don't force. Don't effort. Just release.

Perhaps you send it out with the support of the exhaled breath. Release it in whatever is your way. And if this has created any new spaciousness in your emotion self you expand out the emotional health and wholeness that lives at your core into this newly opened space. You may also wish to partner this with breathing in the larger emotion health and wholeness energy available from the larger universe outside of you. Breathe in and expand out to fill the emotion self with health and wholeness.

You can give this same gift now to your thinking mind. Take time to pause and notice with loving awareness the thoughts and beliefs moving through the mind along with noticing any mental chatter present at this moment of this day.

Pause to notice the thoughts without the need to engage them and perhaps remember that the thoughts are not necessarily your deeper truths. After a few moments of noticing you welcome your thinking mind into this day and this experience. Breathe a breath of acceptance to your mind. And only after noticing, welcoming and extending acceptance do you notice if there are any old beliefs that are no longer true for you or any mental chatter or thoughts that are no longer needed. If there are, and they are ready to be released, you just let them go.

Perhaps with the support of your exhaled breath or whatever is your way. And if this creates any new spaciousness in your mind, you expand out the peace and wholeness that lives at your core to fill this space. Again, you may wish to partner this with the peace and harmony that also lives in the world outside of you. Breathing in and expanding out peace and harmony for the mind.

Now you have created an environment where your wisest Self can emerge. And so you pause and breathe and be as this Self that is your true nature. You take all the time you need deepening your connection as this wise and expansive Self.

You can choose now to remain with your wisest Self in this way or you may choose to go on a journey of turning around the heart.

If you are choosing to go on the journey of turning, you make an inner commitment to the experience. In your mind's eye you find yourself in a safe and pleasant place in nature. You pause appreciating all that is around you.

You become aware of a path that leads to a place of turning. Somehow you know that this place can offer you an opportunity to release some ego limitations, transform perceived weakness into strength, and become even more a conduit of bringing goodness into our world. In your own way and time you begin your exploration of

240

that path. You notice your inner experience as you travel the path. Perhaps you are excited. Perhaps you are a bit fearful. Just notice.

Up ahead you see the opening to a clearing. As you come even nearer you see that others are there in the clearing and you see movement and hear music. Approaching the clearing you decide to enter it. As you enter you choose to sit off to the side with some others.

Sitting in this place you witness the turning of those moving in the center of the circular clearing. They seem graceful and in complete peace in their movements. They turn round and round with no apparent dizziness. From time to time some of those seated with you arise and join the turning. You can choose to remain seated, listening to the music, with no expectation of turning. You may also choose to join the turning. There is no right or wrong only choosing.

Perhaps you spend some time sitting and reflecting on the meaning of the practice of turning for you.

Perhaps you contemplate what ego limitations you might release should you choose to turn. Would you release the inner critic, the need to be right, the insecurity, the fear, what? What gifts might you bring through yourself into our world should you turn? What things about yourself or your life that you have perceived as weaknesses might be ready to be perceived as strength?

Perhaps you just sit enjoying the music.

Perhaps you find yourself moving into a meditative relaxed state.

Perhaps in that state you arise and enter the circle. If you enter that circle you may find yourself moving to the music, moving beyond all limitations, moving as if one with all that is Divine. You release all worry, fear, judgment of self and others. All that remains is the sacred and beautiful. You turn and turn, round and round the heart feeling yourself as the holy gift that you are.

Knowing the others with you are also holy gifts. In your own way you sense the larger energy of Divinity moving through you, in the same way it is moving through the others turning. You notice how this energy ripples out beyond you, beyond those gathered there, beyond the clearing into ever widening circles in our world, and even beyond this world, into the cosmos. You find yourself so grounded in your body and yet so not your body. You are one with everything.

After the perfect amount of time in this clearing, you prepare to depart.

Perhaps you take time first to pause and integrate all that you have experienced.

Perhaps you give gratitude to the others gathered there.

Perhaps you are given a symbol, word or image to take with you to remember your experience. When you are ready, you take a few breaths and once again travel that path back to where you began. Traveling the path this time you notice all the ways that you feel the same or different than when you first came to this path. There is no right or wrong, there is just noticing.

When you arrive back to the beginning of the path, to where you first committed to this journey of turning, you look back and give gratitude for the experience. You now begin to bring your awareness all the way back to where you first began this meditation. You notice your body supported by the surface of where you began the meditation. You take several comfortably deep breaths and, when you are ready, you open your eyes. You give yourself all the time you need before shifting from this meditation to the next part of your day.

You may wish to journal about your experience or share with a trusted friend or companion. In the rest of your day, and in the days to come, you may wish to notice any changes in the way you are experiencing yourself, interacting with others, and experiencing life.

WINDOWS OF POSSIBILITY, CONNECTION, AND TRANSFORMATION

Sometimes we are bombarded with stories of heartache, sorrow, and tragedy. Rodger, a videographer for a local television station, was being exposed to even more than the usual number of tragic news stories. He was also hearing a lot about the gloom and doom, end-of-the-world predictions for 2012. He was feeling overwhelmed and saddened. But Rodger had a plan, a way to highlight a more expanded view of the world. On his off time and with his own equipment, he decided to interview a few people whom he thought might have a broader view. He was particularly interested in their notions and opinions around 2012, and its prophecies and the predictions. Thinking about the ability of YouTube to reach people, he decided to compile interviews for that medium.

When Rodger asked if I would consent to an interview, I agreed. I was humbled by his request but not at all sure I had anything remarkable to offer. In the days leading up to the interviews, I asked for guidance during my daily centering practice about what wanted to be said through me.

When the interview arrived, it became clear that I was nudged to speak to this question: "How do we stay positive, or at least centered, amidst all the negativity and suffering in the world?"

Here is what I shared:

I want to say how much empathy I have for the suffering that is experienced and noticed in the world now and that has been noticed since the beginning of time. Every tradition speaks to that suffering. In the Buddhist tradition, the suffering of the mind is referenced as the 10,000 sorrows (accompanied by 10,000 joys.) It might be called darkness on the altar of the heart that we must sweep clear, in the Sufi tradition. Some Christian traditions speak of something called dark night of the soul. The tradition doesn't really matter. All traditions speak to this human suffering and certainly major world events bring this right up for us; major events in our own lives bring it right up, too! There are no simple answers as to the "whys" of this, though simplistic explanations abound and when those are offered they can seem more like blame rather than explanation. So instead of trying to answer the why, I would like to tell a story.

A women's retreat/workshop drew me to Unity Village, near Kansas City a few years ago. This organization runs a Silent Unity Program designed to offer prayer support. Through this program trained volunteers answer prayer requests via the phones, emails and texts. For more than one hundred and twenty years, they have received prayer requests from all over the world, day and night, numbering in the tens of thousands each month.

These folks are trained to be with those who call for the widest range of concerns and issues. Callers might be suffering from a devastating personal issue or problem, they may be calling on behalf of a loved one, and often the calls come in for global issues or concerns.

The Unity volunteers offer support immediately and then hold the prayer request for thirty days. In their simple chapel, there is a light that is always aglow. It is here that trained people hold vigil twenty-four hours a day, three hundred sixty-five days a year for all of these requests. Volunteers, from one to seven at a time, sit in half-hour shifts holding prayer space for the many intentions.

The original prayers recorded on paper are held in bins or baskets, and are also transferred to a new DVD every day, updating the requests. The actual DVD is visible on a plain, unadorned altar in the chapel. In front of this altar is a wall with a phrase that simply reads, "Peace Be Still."

Ordinarily, only those who have gone through the training are allowed in to the chapel to pray with these intentions. Through a set of circumstances that aren't really important, it evolved that while I was there, two friends and I were allowed to pray with the regular shift volunteers.

First, we were accompanied up a locked elevator to the floor of that chapel whose light can be seen burning brightly from a tower every moment of every day of every year. The door to the chapel is opened only on the half-hour when the next shift of volunteers enters the chapel. We quietly waited, holding sacred silence, for that moment of door opening. I remember my heart beating fast and my breath quickening. I wondered if I would be able to hold that prayer space in the intended way.

Then it was time, and we entered the simple, unadorned chapel in silence. With some anxiety, I sat down in a chair, closed my eyes and went into a prayerful space.

The first thought that entered my mind was, "That's really odd. I don't usually have trouble in most chairs with my feet touching the floor."

Opening my eyes, I looked down and noticed that my feet were indeed touching the floor though it felt that they were floating, buoyant above the floor. I knew in my deepest wisdom that this was a place that can hold a magnitude of concerns and suffering in a way where there is a Higher Buoyancy of love at work, a lifting up if you will, to a higher perspective. The Native Americans might call it the eagle's view.

And so I closed my eyes again, and just entered into a meditative place. This is the image that came to me: A vast, floating banner that looked like gauze covered my entire inner field of vision. It was billowy. It was three-dimensional. It was moving and it was alive.

What became clear, though, was that this gauze-like banner was not made of cotton filaments; like the gauze of first-aid wraps that we bandage wounds in. These threads were filaments of light, luminosity, virtually floating in space. Similar to the little openings in medical gauze, everywhere that two strands of light joined, there was a little window or opening. These windows formed meaningful connections or places of joining. When these intentional and meaning-filled connections formed, windows of possibility were born. This is where expansive wisdom can come through, where new energies can come in, where unknown possibilities, that before we could not see—could not imagine—can make themselves known when we offer ourselves to these meaningful connections.

The Celtic people would call this a "thin place," where a higher perspective can be revealed, realized and accessed. In a way I could understand, I believe I was given a glimpse of the Oneness, that place where we are all connected, that place where possibility lives, a place beyond suffering, a place of the transformation of suffering. I am so amazingly humbled by that glimpse.

And while sometimes my rational, very human mind wants to discount my experience, I know in the deepest fiber of my being what a gift this was and that it was a gift meant to be shared.

When I reflect upon that day, I remember there is a vastness beyond what my small mind can comprehend. There is buoyancy in which even the most unimaginable suffering can be held and transformed.

245

Many great leaders have seen and brought hope among great suffering: Mother Teresa, Jesus Christ, the Buddha and many less famous people. Each teaches us, in their own way, to honor our suffering *and* remember that transformation of suffering is possible. They also teach us that it isn't just the universal, global and external story of suffering that we need to pay attention to; we also need to tend to our own inner and personal story.

Qigong masters say, "I am in the universe and the universe is in me." Mahatma Gandhi, who said, "Be the change you want to see in the world." Thich Nhat Hahn said, "If you want peace, *be* peace."

When we come to that place of suffering, if we become overwhelmed with global issues and feel powerless and insignificant, it helps to remember that for transformation to occur out there, it might just begin with me and then be guided to ripple out in tangible ways to the global issues.

"What is quaking in me? What is toxic in me? What is devastating to me?" Once we identify the suffering in us we can ask, "How can I bring a sense of buoyancy and peace to that first?"

There are many ways that inside me I can create that "silent unity chapel," that place of higher energy to transform: energy work, meditation, prayer, walking in nature, reading the works of people who inspire me, sacred texts, including current poets and authors. How do I come home to that inner chapel within myself?

That's where the inner transformation happens. This doesn't absolve us of acting in a global way. But, it is from that inner chapel place that I can choose how to act to affect the larger system. From that place we can choose how we spend our energy, time, money, support, positivity and hope.

I remember reading somewhere that we may want to notice if we are the kind of person who takes things apart or puts things together. That banner of light, those filaments, is a place where things are put together. I want to be that kind of person who both honors the suffering and puts things together. I want to be the kind of person who offers her light in connection to the light of others, to co-create those places of transformation, those windows of possibility, a place of buoyancy.

Every time we shift to a higher level in our personal consciousness and our global consciousness, there is what is often called devastation. In our history and in the creation stories, we hear this repeatedly. For something new to evolve, something that has been falls away or dissolves. The formation of our planet, Earth, fits this example. We are in such a time of shift now. It is both about honoring how that feels like suffering on a human, personal and global level, *and* remembering, at the same time, the larger story of evolution that's unfolding.

As we honor the suffering it is important to be like the Silent Unity Chapel that can hold amazing suffering, doesn't deny it or pretend it isn't there. Rather, it holds it in a way that transforms it. I think this is what we are called to. When we can hold deep suffering, we can also hold deep joy and lightness.

This is also part of the energy of transformation. This makes me think of the Dali Lama's laugh. During an interview he was asked how he could be enlightened all the time. After a brief pause, he began to laugh. He laughed this amazing, from-the-toes, melodic laugh. Then he told his audience that he isn't enlightened all the time, he has just gotten really, really good at catching himself really, really fast.

He is a man who experiences deep suffering for his people and his country, and a man who can experience great joy along with humility.

Sometimes there are more questions than answers. How do we bring more light? How do we connect our filament of light with someone else's filament of light to create an opening or window for the wisdom and the new possibility to come through? This is a question we may always walk with. We may discover some answers and we may also discover that our answers change over time.

I am seeing more people than ever who are interested in dancing with, embracing and transforming their own suffering and are also willing to dance with, embrace and transform the universal suffering. They want to be an agent of transformation for both.

One favorite passage of mine is "Make Me An Instrument of Your Peace" by Minnesota author, Kent Nerburn.

"We are not saints, we are not heroes. Our lives are lived in the quiet corners of the ordinary. We build tiny hearth fires, sometimes barely strong enough to give off warmth. But, to the person lost in the darkness, our tiny flame may be the road to safety, the path to salvation.

It is not given us to know who is lost in the darkness that surrounds us or even if our light is seen. We can only know that against even the smallest of lights, darkness cannot stand.

A sailor lost at sea can be guided home by a single candle. A person lost in a wood can be led to safety by a flickering flame. It is not an issue of quality or intensity or purity. It is simply an issue of the presence of light."

Mark Nepo, in *The Book of Awakening,* shares a teaching story that speaks about salt in this way. If we took, say, a quarter cup of salt and poured it into a glass of water, it would be much too salty to drink. But if we took the same quarter cup of salt and poured it into a freshwater lake, we could drink that water. When we dilute our bitterness it becomes more palatable.

I believe that there are many sacred places of buoyancy in the world. The Silent Unity Chapel, while incredible, is not the only place.

I believe that the sacred places of holding and transformation reside not just in the outer world.

I believe they reside inside each of us.

I believe we *are* the chapels.

Let's bring our light. Let's be willing to make connection. Let's support each other in honoring the suffering and holding it in a way that can transform it. Let's support the evolution that's here inside of us and all around us. Let's bring a sense of buoyancy. Let's dilute the suffering so we can harvest the gifts we can from it.

So we can move through it as fast as we can. So we can transform it. So we can learn from it what there is to be learned and then share it with each other. Let's do this from the deepest heart and the highest possible light. We are all capable of this. It is not a matter of the intensity or purity or quality of our light. It is simply the presence of light. Let us be that presence of light.

Reflection Questions and Journal Prompts

- *What, if anything, touches you in this story?*

- *What are your stories of being called to do something and then having great doubt? What did you learn about yourself during those times?*

- *Who are your mentors, personal or historic, who have walked with or among great suffering and were able to still carry hope? What are your own stories of this?*

- *What helps you dilute suffering in your life?*

- *Where in your life are places of connection with other threads or strands of light that opened up new windows of possibility that weren't initially present? These might be places of connection with other aspects within you, connections with other people, organizations, or with the Divine. What unfolded from these connections of light?*

- *What supports you in making yourself available to and for such connections?*

- *How do you know that 'chapel' place in you, that place that can hold even great suffering in a way that it can be transformed?*

- *What are your own glimpses of the Oneness where we are all connected?*

- *How are you the presence of light?*

Suggested Activities or Experiences

If there are places of worry in your life, or concerns about global issues, experiment with first identifying the larger issue (famine, war, violence, earthquakes, flooding for example). Then bring that issue to a more personal place of transformation. For example, if the issue is famine you can be with the question, "What places in my life are starving and for what are they starving?" Or if the issue is violence, you could be with the issue in this way, "What places am I allowing violence against myself (self-criticism could be one example) or others (judging others can be a form of violence)."

These are ways of being with the issue in our own life and affecting change where we can. If you do this, just notice how this is for your mind/body/emotion and spirit. Notice if you can bring these issues to an inner place of transformation.

It's very possible that if we all work together in this way, great global change can—and will—happen. We can still take a stand; we can use our energy and money to affect those global issues as well.

Meditation on Being the Chapel of Transformation

Sit or lie down in a place where you won't be interrupted. Close your eyes, if that is comfortable for you. Allow yourself plenty of time to center in the body, mind and emotion self. Make space for the true nature of your expansive self to be present.

Notice your breath as full, soft and easy. Notice your heart and belly softening. Breathe in and out, in and out. Let the breath take you to that place inside you that is the very essence of your light. Nothing to do. Nothing to force or effort. Just let the breath take you to that place inside that is your chapel, that place of buoyancy, that place of honoring suffering and yet awaiting transformation.

That place of connection, of joining the light in you with the larger light of the Oneness. Let your breath help you sink into, rest in that place of possibility, of transformation. And in the silence of this sacred place, let any suffering of mind, body, emotion or spirit that you carry first be noticed and then offered for transformation. In the soft and easy place of the silence, opening now to the windows of new possibility, of new connection and of new transformation.

Pause now, in the silence of your inner chapel, to allow those connections, allow those new windows of possibility, and allow that transformation to unfold. You take all the time you need to be with your own experience in the silence of your inner chapel.

Before you end this meditation, you are given a word, object, symbol or image to take with you to anchor any gifts from this time in the chapel. You also know that you can return to this inner chapel at any time and in any place that you desire.

As you bring your awareness and consciousness back to the location where you began now, you can intend to bring your inner sacred place into even more union with the outer world. You can bring that sacred place of transformation within you even more fully into your day, your work, your play, your relationships, your community, your life, the world and beyond. You can intend to co-create even more buoyant connections, more possibility and transformation right here, right now.

You bring your awareness now back to the place where you first began this meditation. You feel the surface supporting your body. You take several comfortably deep breaths and open your eyes when you

251

are ready. Enter the rest of your day now as that light, as the chapel that you are.

You may wish to journal about your experience or share it with a friend or companion on the journey of life.

AFTERWARD

May you know the power of your own stories
May you mine the precious metals from your own experiences
May the stories that slipped away unnoticed come home
May the stories that have waited to be told find words
May the stories that have been reclaimed find voice
May the stories that have asked to be explored be journeyed
May the healing medicine of your stories find you.
In the spirit of story may you be blessed.

Cindy

(This blessing is in the spirit of John O'Donohue, as in *To Bless the Space Between Us: A Book of Blessing.*)

RESOURCES

Andrews, Ted. *Animal Speak: The Spiritual and Magical Powers of Creatures Great and Small,* St. Paul, Minnesota: Llewllyn Publications, 2004.

Arrien, Angeles. *The Second Half of Life: Opening The Eight Gates of Wisdom,* Boulder, Colorado: Sounds True, 2005.

Chodron, Pema. *Good Medicine: How To Turn Pain into Compassion with Tonglen Meditation.* (DVD). The Pema Chodron Foundation. www.pemachodronfoundation.org or www.shambala.com

Drucker, Karen. Affirming and Inspirational Music and more. www.karendrucker.com

Frost, Seena B. *Soulcollage® Evolving: An Intuitive Collage Process for Self-Discovery and Community,* Santa Cruz, CA: Hanford Mead, 2010.
Also: www.soulcollage.com

Hayes Grieco, Mary. *The Peaceful Heart: A Practical Guide to Unconditional Love and Forgiveness* (CD). www.maryhayesgrieco.com

Laughter Yoga: www.laughteryogaamerica.com

Levine, Stephen. *A Year To Live: How To Live This Year As If It Were Your Last,* New York: Bell Tower, 1997.

Nepo, Mark. *The Book of Awakening: Having The Life You Want By Being Present To The Life You Have,* San Francisco, CA: Conari Press, 2000. Also: www.marknepo.com

Nerburn, Kent. *Make Me An Instrument Of Your Peace: Living In The Spirit Of The Prayer Of Saint Francis,* New York: Harper Collins, 1999.

O'Donohue, John. *To Bless the Space Between Us: A Book of Blessings,* New York: Doubleday, an imprint of The Doubleday Broadway Publishing Group, a division of Random House, Inc., 2008.

Psychosynthesis website: www.two.not2.org/psychosynthesis

Remen, Rachel. *My Grandfather's Blessings: Stories of Strength, Refuge, and Belonging,* New York, New York: The Berkley Publishing Group, A Division of Penguin Putnam Inc., 2000.
Also: www.rachelremen.com

Rumi, Jelaluddin. *The Essential Rumi.* Translated and Compiled by Coleman Barks. San Francisco, CA: Harper, 1997.

Schwartz, Richard C. *Introduction To The Internal Family Systems Model, Oak Park: Trailheads Publications, 2001.*
Also: www.selfleadership.org

Spring Forest Qigong: www.springforestqigong.com

Rodger Routh, videographer: www.rodgerrouth.com

Guy Kyar, illustrator: guykyar@yahoo.com

ACKNOWLEDGEMENTS

The common phrase, "It takes a village" has been said many times, referencing many things. Writing a book is definitely a village process. A book is birthed only with a very expansive group of midwives. I hold deep gratitude and respect for this book's wise, patient, kind and generous midwives.

We are able to read this book in part, because many remarkable people have shared their story experiences with me. I have changed names and other identifying information and, in some cases, formed composite examples to illustrate a theme while still maintaining the integrity of the stories. The sharing and living of your teaching stories is an essential part of this book. You have and continue to inspire me. And now, I suspect, you will be inspiring many others as well. Thank you for your unending generosity.

A cornerstone of this book comes from my mother who taught me the love of books and reading. The love of words was bestowed upon me by my father. Even the last day of his life we were working on the newspaper crossword puzzle. Much love and gratitude to you both.

Joyce Rupp and Mary Kay Shanley, both extraordinary authors, held the space for my first actual writing workshop. The theme of writing from the soul scooped me up and gathered me in. I am still bowing to you both. Thank you for your on-going support.

In life, not to mention in the world of writing, we are extremely fortunate if we have someone who offers critical guidance in a way that keeps our dream alive. Liz Schwab, you have gifted me with this kind of editing guidance and so much more. Your wise and compassionate heart enhanced both this book and my life. It is an honor to know you and call you friend. My gratitude to you and for you is beyond words.

Thank you to Shapato Publishing and Jean Tennant whose patience, wisdom and knowledge has guided this author who had a lot to learn. And gratitude to Betty Taylor who introduced me to Jean.

Gratitude to Guy Kyar for his artistic heart and spirit. Your illustrations have brought added visual life to this book.

I have Rodger Routh to thank for adding his creative spirit to a video summary that speaks to the soul of this book.

Marianne and Barb from Big Red Q Quickprint saved me from my lack of technical expertise more than once. Thanks for all the many ways you contributed to this dream fulfilled.

Karen Drucker, thank you for your inspiration, your encouragement and the most loving kick-in-the-pants I have ever received!

Mudita Sabato, thank you for teaching me how to turn and whirl around the heart. The book title and that story have you to thank.

My supportive midwives, you have listened and listened with care. As good friends and family do, you have held the dream with me. You have offered encouragement when I have been tired or overwhelmed and you have shared in the joy of birthing. Too many to name, I celebrate you, I bow to you, I love you. Without you, these stories might still be waiting for the light of day. And certainly this birth has been much easier and vastly more joyful because of you.

I also want to thank my spiritual community for offering me a place to share teaching stories. You have been a loving and generous audience.

I give endless thanks to—and for—my spouse and life partner, Morgan. You have enhanced my life in immeasurable ways and have given much that I might carry and tend this dream seed to its full birth. Thank you for walking beside me in love and acceptance.

Finally, I thank all the unnamed and unseen guidance in my life and in the lives of us all.

ABOUT THE AUTHOR

Cindy Chicoine is a Licensed Clinical Social Worker, Licensed Massage Therapist and Spiritual Director. She has extensive workshop, group and retreat facilitation experience. In her private practice, in Des Moines, Iowa, Cindy finds inspiration in supporting others in accessing inner wisdom and natural healing potential through individual, small group and workshop/retreat experiences.

Cindy's varied professional training offers a thorough and holistic approach with intentional focus on the mind, emotions, body and spirit. It is her belief that one way we contribute to global change and evolution is by consciously entering our own individual transformative work.

Learn more about Cindy at her website, www.healingpartners.biz.

15782546R00144

Made in the USA
Charleston, SC
20 November 2012